Thoughts

Tools for Practical Living and Building
Better Relationships

Charles E. and Mary A. Sampson

ISBN 978-1-0980-2822-0 (paperback)
ISBN 978-1-0980-2824-4 (hardcover)
ISBN 978-1-0980-2823-7 (digital)

Christian Faith Publishing, Inc.
832 Park Avenue
Meadville, PA 16335
www.christianfaithpublishing.com

Scripture quotations marked (CEV) are from the Contemporary English Version, Second Edition (CEV®) © 2006 American Bible Society. Used by Permission.

Scripture quotations marked KJV are taken from the King James Version of the Bible.

Scripture quotations marked NIV are taken from The Holy Bible, New International Version(R) NIV(R)
Copyright (C) 1973, 1978, 1984, 2011 by Biblica, Inc.(R). Used by permission. All rights reserved worldwide.

Scripture quotations marked NKJV are taken from the New King James Version(R). Copyright 1982 by Thomas Nelson. Used by permission. All rights reserved.

Scripture quotations marked TLB are taken from The Living Bible copyright (c) 1971. Used by permission of Tyndale House Publishers, Inc., Carol Stream, Illinois 60188.
All rights reserved.

The front cover photo by Burlingham/shutterstock.com

Printed in the United States of America

Contents

A Life Remembered

August 7, 2014, Thursday—"I am in a lot of pain, my lower back is really hurting, along my stomach. I am nauseated too. I am having a mellow day enjoying the sunshine as my body is shutting down, and I am thanking God."

—An excerpt taken from Carisa's journal from the book/booklet that my wife and I have written with the aid of Edwina Frazier, Publishing Consultant-Partners In Success Publishing. The book is titled, *A Life Remembered.*

Carisa Nicole
Jacquette Sampson

We would like to dedicate this book to our daughter, the late Carisa Nicole Jacquette Sampson. The following paragraphs are taken from a chapter of the, A Life Remembered book/booklet. Carisa was the victim of a stroke at the age of thirty-nine. The stroke occurred on **Sunday**, **September 26, 2010**. It left her paralyzed on the entire left side of her body. Along with the stroke, Carisa had multiple complex medical conditions. Her extensive medical issues included congestive heart failure; left ventricular cardiomyopathy; spinal stenosis; gastroparesis; chronic back, hip, and neck pain; insulin dependency; diabetes complications; chronic kidney disease; and neuropathy. If these weren't bad enough, due to the diabetic complications, her left eyeball had to be removed. Also, all of her teeth were removed. Subsequently, Carisa passed on **September 8, 2014**, at the age of forty-three due to kidney failure.

TEAM CARISA

Seated: Carisa, Back Row L to R: Charles (Dad),
Jacoby (Son), Cedric (Brother)
The first of *Seven* Gold Medals

Carisa was a great inspiration to the family and all of those who came in contact with her as she courageously battled multiple medical conditions. She inspired and touched many people in her life and in death. Carisa lived her life with zest and fulfillment through the final transition. She didn't view her stroke and medical issues as the end of her life. Instead of sulking in self-pity or sorrow, she simply saw them as an opportunity for God to prove himself and get the glory as he gave her strength to endure the pain and suffering while he prepared her to face death.

Carisa did not complain or ask, "Why me?" She did not feel sorry for herself nor did she allow others to feel sorry for her. She often took the time to check on or visit (via the access bus) other family members and friends. Her conversations were always positive. She enjoyed encouraging others and lifting their spirits despite the severe pain she experienced twenty-four hours a day. Helping them helped her. Carisa also encouraged family members and friends, whether it was verbal, sending letters or upbeat notes.

Carisa constantly said that she was going to live her life to the fullest and enjoy it until God pulled the plug. *And that she truly did!* In 2013, Carisa joined the Renton Roadrunners and represented them in the Washington State Special Olympics. She was an inspiration to her coaches and teammates. Between 2013 and 2014, Carisa won *seven* gold medals and *one* silver medal in the Softball Individual Wheelchair Division and Track and Field Competition in the Wheelchair Division. She looked beyond the constant pain, paralysis, and other medical challenges while death was imminent and lived the last four years of her life with zest.

Carisa valiantly prepared her family and friends for the inevitable and wanted us to be at peace with her decision not to prolong life through dialysis. She wasted no time on what could have been and focused on the reality of the day to day life, which she was determine to live with zest, until the Lord took her home. She met with us separately, first meeting with her son, Jacoby, her immediate family, then relatives, and friends. Her message was that she was tired, had made peace with God, and was ready to go be with him. She assured us that she was at peace and didn't want us to be sad for her because she was ready to go. Carisa, with the aid of her mother (my wife), begun to plan her funeral about six months prior to her death. She called several people and asked them to deliver her story at the funeral. Also, she called a relative, requesting her to sing at the funeral.

Carisa had tremendous faith in God, her words were, "My life is in God's hand, and who wouldn't serve a God like that!" She also made it plain that she was totally committed to serving God. Despite all the calamities Carisa experienced, she would often say, **"I have a good life."** Her favorite quote was, "My destination (heaven) is greater than my dilemma (medical problems)."

Carisa won her seventh and final gold medal on *August 16, 2014* (about three weeks before she passed). A week before the competition, Carisa said, "I am going to the Special Olympics Competition and win my last gold medal, and then I'm going home (her heavenly home)." Carisa addressed the prediction to Cindy Bonilla, the Director of Occupational Therapist, at Full Life Adult Day Health Center, located in Seattle, Washington. Carisa and Cindy shared mutual admiration.

Carisa did win her seventh and final gold medal as she predicted, and shortly thereafter, went home, as she also predicted.

We are so proud of our daughter, Carisa Nicole Jacquette Sampson. She inspired us so much. Carisa left a lasting imprint on many people with her positive attitude despite the adversities and chronic pain she faced every day. With God's help, Carisa skillfully played the hand dealt to her. She faced death head-on without any hesitation as she patiently waited for it to come to go be with the Lord, to never, never suffer again!

A Life Remembered is a very inspirational, testimonial book/booklet that captures the last four years of Carisa's life as she courageously met insurmountable medical challenges head on without backing down as she put all her trust in the Lord. I have no doubt this book/booklet will be an inspirational reading. Your life will not be the same after reading it. The cost of the booklet is $10.00 and can be purchased by going to Carisa's website at: https://carisa.homesteadcloud.com. You can also view comments left by others who purchased the book.

The **Seven** and *Final* Gold Medal Captured—August 16, 2014

Preface

I would like to thank my wife, Mary, for supporting me in all aspects during the writing of this book. Mary's middle name is Alice, her parents addressed her as Mary Alice. So, it came as no surprise that others followed suit and preferred calling her Mary Alice opposed to Mary. So with that being said, from this point forward throughout the book, Mary will be referred to as Mary Alice. Also, I would like to acknowledge my son Cedric, grandson Jacoby, granddaughters Janahya and Imani, and great-granddaughter Harmoney. You have been strong influences in my life. Special thanks to Jacoby, Imani, my Brother, Lee Sampson, my Sister, Corinthia F. Sampson, friend, Bobby W. Outley, Brother-in-Law, Willie E. Manning, friend, Joyce Hanspard-Hewitt, and Stephanie Fife for your inputs in this book. I would also like to thank my siblings, nieces and nephews, in-laws, their families, friends who supported me during the good times and stood alongside me in my bleakest hours. A thank you to Christian Faith Publishing for publishing my book, and my Publication Specialist, Tiffany Minter for her diligence in assisting me to ensure the book would be completed to my satisfaction. Special thanks to my Brother-in-Law, John E. Manning for suggesting the title to our book.

I was inspired to write this book from the encouragement of my wife's cousin, Willie Lee "Josh" Manning. Josh suggested I write a book that contains proverbs and parables. Josh came up with this concept after reading material that I've written and from listening to the proverbs and parables I used when mediating or giving advice. He felt the book would encourage many and be a tool for enhancing their lives.

I pondered Josh's suggestion for a few months and thought to myself, *Why not do it, especially if it could be a blessing in helping some-one? Even if only one person is encouraged and inspired after reading this book, then it would be worth it.* So I decided to take Josh's suggestion and write this book.

Through my own personal life experiences, good or bad, highs or lows, also while observing and talking to others about their good or bad experiences, I was blessed to present simple solutions to solve most problems. In any given situation wisdom has taught me to analyze, dissect and reduce the problem to the simplest solution.

The Dirty Dozen

I retired from the Seattle Police Department as a Community Service Officer (CSO) after thirty-seven years. The Community Service Officers Unit was created as a pilot project. During this time, unrest existed between the African American Community and the Seattle Police Department/Police Officers. The majority of the African Americans resided in the Central District, also called, the Central Area or the C.D. The Black Panthers Party office was located in the C.D. at the time.

The mission of the CSOs was to be a Liaison between the Police Department and the African American Community. In December 1971 the first twelve Community Service Officers were hired. The twelve consisted of eleven African Americans (9 males and 2 females) and one Caucasian male. The task for the African Americans CSOs seemed to be the most challenging. It appeared that we were a bunch of misfits. I say this because we weren't accepted by most of the Caucasian Police Officers, the rumor was they felt we were a threat to their job security. I would not rule out that prejudice lurked deep within. On the other hand, we weren't accepted by a majority of the African American Community, they labeled us as, *Traitors, Uncle Toms,* and *Snitches.* They disliked the Caucasian CSO simply because he was "White."

Since the seemly insurmountable challenges set before us was extremely daring, perhaps we should have been referred to as The **Dirty Dozen**. Similar to the 1967 movie, *The Dirty Dozen,* starring Lee Marvin, Jim Brown, Telly Savalas, Donald Sutherland, Ernest Borgnine, Charles Bronson and so on. During World War II, a US Army Major, John Reisman (role played by Lee Marvin) was assigned to handpick twelve convicted murderers to train and successfully lead them on a mission that took them deep into enemy territory. The mission involved assassinating German Officers.

Just as The Dirty Dozen was successful in their mission, I am proud to say that we were successful in accompanying the difficult task assigned to us. Over a period of time the CSO unit bridged the gap between the African American Community and the Seattle Police Department/Police Officers. Because of the success, the Community Service Officer Unit was implemented into the Seattle Police Department budget, subsequently additional CSOs were hired. The CSOs handled all non-law enforcement service calls for the Police Department. We handled 911 dispatched calls, calls from citizens via landline or walk-ins. Counseling and Conflict Mediation were some of the services we provided. To ensure we were well-equipped to assist the parties in coming to a win-win solution, CSOs received ongoing intense diverse training and attended many seminars. The training and seminars were an asset. Also, it taught me ways to come up with simple solutions in solving complex problems. I apply the knowledge I acquired in solving conflicts to my life. The training enabled me to assist others in resolving their problems.

Come Now, Let Us Reason Together

The purpose of this book is to assist, encourage, and inspire others in practical living and building better relationships. The practical thoughts, proverbs and parables found in this book will prompt you to think and then realize that for every problem, there is a simple fix. Once the problem is broken down, you will discover that it is not as complex as it seemed to be.

Some of the practical thoughts, proverbs and parables in this book may generate debates, disagreements, heated arguments, or other negative reactions, but that's not our intent nor is it the purpose of this book. Our desire is that the practical thoughts, proverbs and parables would initiate a dialogue.

I will take the time and provide a crash course on a dialogue versus a debate. The difference between a dialogue and a debate is as follows: a dialogue is harmonious, two or more people working toward a common understanding. A debate is contradictory, two or more people opposing each other in an attempt to prove the other wrong. In a dialogue, one listens to another's point of view to find agreement.

In a debate, one listens in hopes of finding a weakness, to strengthen their argument. In a dialogue, one listens to the other side(s) for clarity, to seek answers, solutions, and to get a different perspective. In a debate, one is stuck on their point of view, there's only one right answer and they have it. In a dialogue, one chooses their words carefully not to offend the other party(s). In a debate, one is inconsiderate of the other party's feelings. They would often take jabs, or criticize the other person(s). In a dialogue, finding a common ground or a win-win solution is the goal. In a debate, winning is the goal. In a dialogue, keeping an open mind for better understanding is the goal. In a debate, the mind remains closed, conclusion is drawn, and a determination to be right is the goal. Dialogues brings unity, while debates create alienation, and alienation leads to loneliness.

I have witnessed many heated debates based on opinions. An opinion is nothing but thoughts or belief that is not supported by facts. If you don't agree with another person's opinion, it is better to say "I disagree" instead of saying "You're wrong," unless you have the facts to back it up. Disagreeing simply means you don't share the same belief or point of view as the other party or parties. Now, having said that, it doesn't necessarily mean what is being said is right, wrong, or indifferent. It just means you don't agree with what is being said.

So Close—Yet So Far Away

Since I'm a resident of Washington State, I will use the Seattle Seahawks football team as an example. I witnessed two or more people get into heated debates about the Seahawks making it to the Super Bowl. The debate began to heat up as they got into a yelling match where one side is screaming at the other side, telling them they were wrong and that the Seahawks will not make it to the Super Bowl. The Super Bowl's contenders is yet to be determined, and no one knows which team will qualify to participate. So that being the case, no one is right or wrong. It's just opinions. On the other hand, if the other party or parties argue that the Seahawks have never won a Super Bowl, then the opposing party can tell them they are indeed wrong, and the information is incorrect since it could be backed up with facts because on *February 2, 2014*, the Seattle Seahawks were Super Bowl *XLVIII* (48) Champions, which ended the *2013 season*. The Seahawks defeated the Peyton Manning led Denver Broncos' High-Powered Offense by a whooping score of 43-8.

On a side note: the Seahawks should have been back-to-back Super Bowl Champions as well if only they would have given the ball to Marshawn Lynch with less than one yard from pay dirt gold (and bragging rights for the Washingtonians), in Super Bowl XLIX (49) against the New England Patriots. I'm sure the whole world holds that belief. I'm not sure if I would ever get **"past"** that missed opportunity. Having said that, there is no guarantee or proof Marshawn Lynch would have scored, or that the Seattle Seahawks would have won the Super Bowl, so with that being said, it all boils down to an opinion. The fact is that the New England Patriots won the game and was crowned the Super Bowl Champion, *end of story.*

Now back to my aforementioned point regarding opinions and facts. The same holds true here. If the thoughts, proverbs and parables in this book are not backed by facts of your personal life experiences, then treat it as an opinion, and don't get drawn into heated debates because it has no merit.

In this book, you will find, for the most part, that there are no right or wrong answers. A person's answer or opinion will most likely be based on their personal past or present experience. To some, the practical thoughts and parables found in this book will be a matter of fact, and to others, they will be a matter of perception. It all boils down to an individual's life experience. I repeat: the comments or opinions will vary. There are no right or wrong answers. As the saying goes, "There is an exception to every rule," The same holds true in some of the thoughts, proverbs and parables found in this book. Enjoy your reading.

Affirmation Statements

POSITIVE THINKING IS:

1. The complete opposite of negative thinking.
2. The antidote for negative thinking.
3. Taking ownership of your thoughts and behavior, while at the same time holding yourself accountable.
4. Not wishful thinking.
5. Thinking positive, when thinking positive seems to be foolish.
6. When you can see a ray of sunshine at the end of the tunnel despite the bright lights from the fast-approaching train.
7. If the answer is always, "I can," when insurmountable circumstances say, "You cannot."
8. Acknowledging, recognizing and being convince that the phrase "I can't, or I cannot" is abstract, and not a substitute for saying, "I *choose not*, to do a certain thing."
9. When you can view obstacles as a stepping stone and proceed, instead of a roadblock and retrieve.
10. When you embrace adversities, realizing it's only a tool for growth and building character.
11. Looking beyond the worse and seeing the good in every individual and every situation, every single time.
12. Being confident of a good outcome when the odds are 99.9 percent against you.
13. Setting goals and giving yourself permission to accomplish them.
14. Defining yourself and being content with the definition.
15. Not seeing falling short of set goals as a sign of failure but a challenge to work harder.
16. Enduring the storms while reaching for the sunshine.

17. Being well aware that you don't have it all and recognizing that it takes every piece to make the puzzle complete.
18. When you know there's a bright side in every difficult situation and continuing to look until you find it.
19. Understanding that no matter how bad the problem is, it could always be worse.
20. Appreciating what you have and not complaining about what you don't have.
21. Understanding you will not win every battle but also will not be defeated, so keep fighting.
22. Accepting a setback as nothing but a setup to better things ahead that await you.
23. When you are positive that **positive** thinking **will** bring positive results every single time.
24. Having the assurance that adversities, disappointments, heartaches, and heartbreaks are necessary tools to enhance mental and spiritual growth.
25. Being convinced that giving up is not an option.
26. Looking beyond the unpleasant circumstances and grasping the desired outcome.
27. Having the courage to snatch joy and happiness from the jaws of despair, disappointments and hopelessness.
28. Believing and trusting that God is able to do what we cannot.
29. Is thinking positive when positive thinking doesn't seem to be an option.
30. **Is never, never, ever giving up!**

choose joy

Words to live by...

Today I *Choose* Joy...

Every day, I have a choice

as to how I view my day and my circumstances.

I get to choose joy even in the painful seasons.

I get to choose love even in upset.

I get to choose light, even in darkness.

In my choice to BE *love*...

I get to be a light for others to see hope.

So in every minute...

I get to *choose.*

I *choose* to shine.

I *choose* to be a light.

I *choose* to be love.

I *choose* to BELIEVE.

...and in these choices

my heart is filled with *joy.*

~Stephanie Fife

"I can do all things through Christ which strengtheneth me."

Philippians 4:13 (kjv)

The Battle Continues

For every action, there is a reaction, whether it's positive or negative. For every positive thought, within a split-second, negative thoughts will automatically follow. For every good deed one does, evil thoughts are also present. As mortals, we cannot prevent this from occurring for it is the law of the flesh.

The Apostle Paul said, "For I know that in me (that is, in my flesh,) dwelleth no good thing... For the good that I would I do not: but the evil which I would not, that I do... I find then a law, that, when I would do good, evil is present with me" (Rom. 7:18a, 19, 21, KJV).

Flip the Switch

As believers, we cannot prevent evil (negative) thoughts from surfacing, but we most certainly can change the process when they attempt to enter our minds. Someone may ask, "How is this possible, knowing that we are in the flesh and are mere human beings?"

The obvious Christian answer is, "With God, all things are possible." But, in layman's terms, the answer to the question is we must first change the way we think. To change a behavior (acceptable or unacceptable), we must change the way we think about the behavior or what we thought we saw, whether it be a bad situation or a good behavior.

Just as very large vessels such as an eighteen-wheeler truck, automobiles, ships, and the like are controlled by such a small object as a steering wheel or helm (on ships), our minds and bodies are controlled by how we process the thoughts that enter the mind. "*Positive* thoughts beget positive results and makes a happy person." But on the contrary, "*Negative* thoughts beget negative results and makes a miserable person." It was once said, "Misery loves company." The good news is it doesn't have to be you or me. No one is required to accept the invitation to misery's party.

How important is it to maintain positive thoughts? Positive thoughts are very good nourishment for the mind, soul, spirit, and body. Positive thought unites. On the other hand, negative thoughts are destructive to the mind, soul, spirit, and body. Positive thoughts are always constructive, while constantly harboring negatives thoughts are just the opposite. They are destructive and can also destroy good relationships. When the negative thoughts enter our minds, simply flip the switch to positive thinking.

In Philippians 4:8, Paul exhorts the believers to maintain positive thoughts by thinking on: whatsoever is true, honest, just, pure, lovely, and of good report. These are all positive, healthy thoughts.

It is impossible to have a happy soul with a corrupt, negative-thinking mindset. *You are who you think you are and not who others say and think you are. The person that defines you is the same person who validates you, and their validation may not be accurate. I have made a practice of maintaining a positive outlook when the times are bleak. I must admit it is a challenge to do so. There are times when I allow doubts to surface, but I try to quickly distinguish them and flip the switch.*

You Are Who You Think You Are

As I said earlier, you are who you think you are and not who or what others think you should be. Proverbs 23:7a (KJV) says, "For as he thinketh in his heart, so is he."

If you can't see far, then you won't go far. In other words, one must be able to look beyond what the naked eyes can see to reach their maximum potential. Visualizing is very important in this process, for *visualization* plays a great role in a person's *motivation, determination,* and finally their destination.

Off to See the Wizard

I will explore four of the characters in *The Wizard of Oz* movie as an example to further make my point. They are Dorothy, the Tin Man, the Scarecrow, the Lion and the Wizard. In the story, **all** except the Wizard felt they lacked something that would make them complete. For the Tin Man, it was a heart, the Scarecrow wanted a brain, the Lion wanted courage, and of course Dorothy only wanted to go back home to Kansas. As for Dorothy's dog, Toto, he didn't ask for anything. He was content being loved by Dorothy. So they decided to travel to the Land of Oz to see the Wizard in hopes of getting their needs met or perhaps to get validated at the least.

Upon arriving in Oz, and learning of the Wizard's deceptions of the true person hiding behind the curtain, Dorothy rebuked him. Perhaps out of guilt, the Wizard granted their requests by giving symbolic gifts to the three of them.

He gave the Tin Man a small heart-shaped clock, representing a heart. The Tin Man heard the clock ticking and became excited and saw it as a confirmation that he indeed had a heart. Perhaps he understood each tick from the clock as a sign of a heartbeat.

The Scarecrow received a diploma with the words, Honorary Degree of Th.D. (Doctor of Thinkology) written on it. He felt that the diploma validated his status. This gave the Scarecrow confidence. He felt because of the degree he was intelligent; therefore had a brain.

To the Lion, the Wizard gave a medal, citing it was the Triple Cross Medal. The Lion was then initiated as a member into the Legion of Courage Club by the Wizard. The medal had the word "Courage" written on it. As a result, the Lion wore the medal with pride. After all, he was no more a coward but a brave Lion and could now live up to his name as the King of the Jungle and had a Medal of Bravery to prove it.

There's No Place Like Home

Dorothy was not given a symbolic object to represent her home. Her only option was to visualize being home. In her mind, she could see the home that she left in Kansas as she continued to repeat, "There's no place like home, there's no place home, there's no place like home…" She continued to repeat the saying until she believed it from the depths of her soul. Before she realized it, she was back home in Kansas with her lovely family.

We must do as Dorothy did when the obstacles seem to be impossible to overcome. We must continue to say it until we believe it. Subsequently, it will become a reality. *There will be times in our life when we will need to separate ourselves from the negativity and focus on the good things. Believers must continue to think positive and trust in the Word of God until we believe it without a shadow of doubt. Every so often we must be prepared to encourage ourselves and depend less on others for support. We must continue to think positive when circumstances dictate otherwise. The Scripture says, "Save yourselves from this untoward [corrupt] generation" (Acts 2:40a, KJV).*

Dorothy, the Tin Man, the Scarecrow, and the Lion were so elated that the Wizard gave them exactly what they wanted. But did he, really? The diploma, medal, and the heart-shaped clock were only symbolic—nothing more, nothing less—but seeing it convinced them they were what the object represented. For the Lion, he instantly became brave, and the Scarecrow suddenly received a brain and became intelligent as a result. The Tin Man was happy for his new clock or, should I say, brand-new heart given by the Wizard, and Dorothy was back home with the family she loved. I concur with Dorothy: There is never any place like home. Home is more than a physical structure but a place where you can find love, peace, and happiness.

In each situation, the only thing the Wizard did was aid them in changing the negative thoughts they had and turned them into positive thinking. The positive thoughts changed their mindset and behaviors to a brighter outlook. As for Dorothy, she repeated the saying "There's no place like home," until she believed it, or spoke it into existence. *There are times in our lives when we should be like Dorothy. If things are not what we like for them to be, we should continue to say it 'til we believe it.* The story had a happy ending. Each one received exactly what they were seeking. Even though they possessed it before taking the long journey to Oz.

I don't want to minimize the important role the **Wizard** played in Dorothy and her friends' lives. He couldn't give them what they wanted because they already possessed it. But he provided them with what they needed, and that was confidence to believe in themselves. To some, this was achieved by symbolic objects presented by the Wizard. He helped them to realize that the greatest reason for their failure is not caused by the opposition on the outside, but by the unsafe belief that controlled them on the inside.

At one time or another we all had or have wizards in our lives, whether they be parents, grandparents, brothers, sisters, aunts, uncles, other relatives, friends, school teachers, ministers, counselors, and so forth. A wizard is a mentor or someone who encouraged and assisted you in reaching your full potential. Every successful person was blessed to have at least one wizard in their life. Without the Wizard, fake as he was, perhaps, neither Dorothy, the Tin Man, the Lion, or the Scarecrow would have reached their desired goal.

Another lesson to be learned from this story is that every single person possesses a unique gift that can make a difference in another person's life. One should never, never, ever look down on or condescendingly speak to another. Everybody has something to offer—no exceptions. The person who is rejected just may be the only person who can help in your time of desperate needs.

Lookin' Outward for What You Already Have Within

It's unfortunate that Dorothy, the Tin Man, the Lion, and the Scarecrow felt that it was necessary to make the long journey to Oz in order to obtain what they already had but didn't realize it was already there. The Lion was brave. It was well-known that he was the King of the Jungle at birth. The Tin Man had a heart. Perhaps he cried long before he met the Wizard, indicating he had emotion and compassion, which further indicated that he had a heart. In my recollection of the movie, the **Scarecrow** was smart. He made some wise and intelligent decisions on his way to see the Wizard. Aside from that, how could he frighten others away by deception: allowing them to believe that he was a real person instead of straw wrapped in clothes if he didn't have a brain?

As for Dorothy, well, as you could see from the movie she never left home as she thought. It was all the negative thoughts that entered into her mind, as well as her friends and took control over the rest of their bodies, which caused them to react in a negative manner. Of course, the movie depicted Dorothy as having a bad dream. However, many mistake a dream for reality and act on it whether the dream be good or bad. Ecclesiastes 5:3 (CEV) says, "If you keep thinking about something, you will dream about it. If you talk too much, you will say the wrong thing." However, some dreams have a valid purpose. Throughout the Bible, you will find that God spoke to many people through dreams.

There are times when one may travel far, spending a great amount of time, energy and a large sum of money to discover what they were looking for or needed, they already possessed it. The positive spin on obtaining it in that manner is if they were able to stumble upon it, then it was well worth the trip and should be viewed as a much-needed learning experience. In some cases, it may be imperative that we hit rock bottom as a wake-up call in order for us to realize how great we are.

Oh, let's not forget about Toto, the terrier, and the role he played. Toto was Dorothy's adorable dog. Dorothy loved him dearly. Toto symbolized "loyalty" and "trust." No matter how dim the situation looked, Dorothy was never forsaken by Toto. He trusted her to protect him and provide the things of necessity even though she had her own issues.

Positive Thoughts

"I can" is a very positive statement! We can do a lot more than we think, but when we say, "I can't do this or that," we're already defeated before we get started. However, I realized that there are things that are out of our realm or capacity that we cannot do.

I remember when I was a fifth-grade student at St. Charles Catholic Colored Elementary School. The school was located in West Monroe, Louisiana. One of the students asked the nun/teacher if he could go outside. The nun's response was, "You *can* go outside, but you *may* not." As a fifth-grader, the nun's response confused me, "You can, but you may not!" *What is she talking about? That makes no sense*, I thought to myself. My thoughts were not verbalized for obvious reasons. A student dare not challenge the Nuns, this one in particular.

But soon her reply shed the light on my childhood thinking. It made a lot of sense. The nun went on to explain to the student what she meant by "You can, but you may not." She explained that in the content of her response, "**can** is defined as having the ability to do a certain thing, and **may** is defined as having permission to do a certain thing." She added, "You certainly have the ability to go outside, but I'm not giving you the permission to go outside." I learned a valuable lesson that day. As you can see, the nun's succinct explanation stuck with me.

When we say that we can do a certain thing, we are saying that we have the ability and are able to do it. This empowers us to complete the task, but when we say we cannot, then we can't, and will not attempt to do it. This sort of thinking only sets us up for failure. But if we say, "I can do it but choose not to do it," then what we're saying is, "I'm in complete control over the situation, I have the ability to do it, and the decision to do it or not is in my full control or power."

The Holy Ghost, the Life
Changer, and Life Sustainer

Why is the baptism of the Holy Ghost essential to believers? Jesus said in John 14:26 (KJV, emphasis added), "But the Comforter, which is the Holy Ghost, whom the Father will send in my name, he shall teach you all things, and bring all things to your remembrance, whatsoever I have said unto you." Let me say this: in order for one to make a cash withdrawal, there must first be a deposit." No one can get anything from your account (even with your authorization) if there's nothing there. **"Nothing in, nothing out."**

My point is that believers must *read, believe,* and *receive* the Word of God. *Once it is received* (deposited), then the Holy Ghost will help you to rightly divide (withdraw) it and give you the discernment and wisdom to apply the Word of God. He will also bring it (the Word) to your remembrance at the appropriate time.

The Twelve Disciples walked with Jesus for approximately three and a half years. They had not received the baptism of the Holy Ghost at the time, and as a result, they were carnal-minded and could not fully comprehend the message Jesus was trying to impart to them. Because of that, Jesus was limited in the depth he could go with them.

But oh boy! When they received the Holy Ghost, it was a totally different ball game. It made a tremendous difference. Not only were they able to proclaim the Word with power; but the Holy Ghost also quickened their minds by bringing back to their remembrance the things Jesus was trying to get through to them. Only then were they able to understand the complete message Jesus was trying to convey to them. They were able to deliver the message with power and conviction.

Jesus added, "Howbeit when he, the Spirit of truth, is come, he will guide you into all truth: for he shall not speak of himself; but whatsoever he shall hear, that shall he speak: and he will **shew** you things to come" (John 16:13, KJV, emphasis added).

The Word of God is true. "You shall know the truth and the truth will most definitely make you free" (John 8:32). I was told that no one operates by the whole truth but the truth they perceive it to be. If that is true, then what is truth? Someone may ask. The answer is found in the Scripture. Jesus said in John 14:6 (KJV, emphasis added), "I am the way, the *truth*, and the life: no man cometh unto the Father, but by me."

Is it a Delusion or a Foregone Conclusion?

The Word of God is precious. Once you receive it, hold on to it and guard it with your heart because your life (spiritual life) will depend on it. You will most certainly die without it (spiritual death). Be wise, lest the Adversary deceives you into believing a fake doctrine. However, the Spirit will let you know if the doctrine is the real deal or a carbon copy. It may look and sound like the real thing, but in actuality, it's only a fake version of sanctification.

Even Jesus was not immune from the devil's deceptive tactics. Jesus is **the Word** and the master of **the Word**, yet the devil tried to use the Scripture on Him in the wilderness (Luke 4:9–11). Not to be undone, Jesus, being the Word, put the Word back on the devil. Jesus response was, "It is said, thou shall not tempt the Lord thy God." (Luke 4:12, KJV). When the devil finally realized that his tactics were futile and could not get Jesus to bend, sway or break, he fled, but only for a season. The devil uses the same tactic today in an attempt to discredit the Word of God. He create debates and misinterpretation of the Holy Bible and causes many to rely on their intellect, philosophy, or their own opinions instead of relying on the Holy Ghost to lead and guide them in all truth. "The letter kills, but the Spirit gives life" (2 Cor. 3:6a, NKJV). The same can be said in a different way. It goes like this: "The old way, trying to be saved by keeping the Ten Commandments, ends in death; in the new way, the Holy Spirit gives them life" (2 Cor. 3:6, TLB).

It is of the utmost importance that believers refrain from entertaining any form of teaching that is contrary to what the Word of God says, no matter how true or convincing it may sound. Cleave to the truth. Let no one lead you astray with enticing words. Paul told the Galatian Christians that if anyone, (themselves included) even an angel from heaven preaches any other gospel other than the one they preached unto them, let them be cursed (Gal. 1:8).

The Disguised Lies Encountered, The Transparency Truth

From the beginning of time in the Garden of Eden, the devil took the Word of God and twisted it to suit his evil purpose. He told Eve she would surely not die as God said she would if she ate the fruit of the tree that was located in the middle of the garden. The devil proceeded to tell Eve that God knew if she ate the fruit, her eyes would be opened, and she would be as gods, knowing good and evil (Genesis 3:5, KJV). In essence, the devil was telling Eve that God was not being truthful and trying to hold her back or prevent her from reaching her full potential of being somebody important. He made it sound so genuine and appetizing until it caused her to veer from the truth, (the Word of God) and convinced her husband, Adam to do likewise, to join the disobedient club, where Satan is the founder. Word of caution, whenever the devil tell or suggest we do or not do a certain thing, no matter how authentic it may sound, do the opposite. His sole mission is to persuade us to disobey God, and to destroy humanity by any and all insidious means necessary.

Warning alert! When the serpent/devil called God a liar, Eve should have abruptly ended the conversation and removed herself from his presence. There's nothing else to discuss. Likewise, if we are discussing the Bible or witnessing, if anyone calls God or His Word a lie (as the devil said to Eve), it doesn't matter if it come from the pulpit or the Sinners' Elite Club (if there were such a club), you should immediately shut down the conversation, unless the Holy Spirit leads you to proceed. Debating the Word of God is not an option for believers. It only causes animosity or sows discord (disharmony/quarreling).

The devil is yet again doing today as he did to Eve in the beginning of creation. When the Word of God (affirmation, *a positive statement*) goes out, the devil quickly tries to discredit or nullify it by declaring there is *no value, importance,* or *consequences* for disobeying

God's word. He knows **the Word** is powerful enough to deliver souls from his grasp. I will share some examples of affirmation statements from the Word of God and nullification responses from the devil and those who possess similar spirits. Let the conversation begin!

Jesus: "All that the Father giveth me shall come to me: and him that cometh to me: I will in no wise cast out." (John 6:37, KJV)

The Devil: Yeah right! Only if you meet his high standards. Just watch and see what will happen when you fall below his high expectations and standards.

Jesus: "A new commandment I give unto you. That you love one another: as I have loved you, that ye also love one another." (John 13:34, KJV)

The Devil: As if the ten (Commandments) weren't enough. He had to add another one. You are well aware that I don't command or demand anything of you. I merely offer suggestions, with a little persuasion, and allow you to make your own decisions with no strings attached.

Jesus: "And ye shall be hated of all men for my name's sake: but he that endureth to the end shall be saved." (Matt. 10:22, KJV)

The Devil: You see, that's the difference between him and me. People will hate **him** because of what he forces you to do, but on the other hand, they will hate **you**, and not **me**, when you do what I merely suggest.

Jesus: "But take heed to yourselves: for they shall deliver you up to councils: and in the synagogues, ye shall be beaten: and ye shall be brought before rulers and kings for my sake, for a testimony against them." (Mark 13:9, KJV)

The Devil: Guilty by association! He's a poor example for a leader. I will never allow that to happen to you.

Jesus: "If the Son therefore shall make you free, ye shall be free indeed." (John 8:36, KJV)

***The Devil*: Liar! Liar! Liar!** How can you feel free when you have to tiptoe around all those impossible rules he forces you to live by?

Jesus: "Ye are of your father the devil, and the lusts of your father ye will do. He was a murderer from the beginning, and abode not in the truth, because there is no truth in him. When he speaketh a lie, he speaketh of his own: for he is a liar, and the father of it." (John 8:44, KJV)

***The Devil*:** Wow! Low blow. He's now playing "the dozen," just because you choose not to be a part of his family.

Jesus: "Then spake Jesus again unto them saying, 'I am the light of the world.'" (John 8:12a, KJV)

***The Devil*:** Big Deal! And I am the prince of the air and the master of darkness as well. I have many secret hiding places that he doesn't have a clue.

Jesus: "I pray not that thou shouldest take them out of the world, but that thou shouldest keep them from the evil. They are not of the world, even as I am not of the world." (John 17:15–16, KJV)

***The Devil*:** And I own the world. Need I say more?

Jesus: "Come unto me, all ye that labour and are heavy laden, and I will give you rest." (Matt. 11:28, KJV)

***The Devil*:** I also have many options to provide you with R & R (rest and relaxation) whenever I feel you need to take a break.

Jesus: "Think not that I am come to send peace on earth. I came not to send peace, but a sword. For I am come to set a man at variance against his father, and the daughter against her mother, and the daughter in law against her mother in law. And a man's foe shall be they of his own household." (Matt. 10:34–36, KJV)

***The Devil*:** Now do you believe me? For centuries, I have been telling you that he really doesn't care about you. He is a troublemaker and a homewrecker. You all were doing just fine until he butted into our business.

Jesus: "The thief cometh not, but for to steal, and to kill, and to destroy: I am come that they might have life, and that they might have it more abundantly." (John 10:10, KJV)

The Devil: The keyword **"might"** sounds sort of iffy. If his life is so fantastic and something to die for, then why doesn't he guarantee it?

Jesus: "Beware of the false prophets, which come to you in sheep's clothing, but inwardly they are ravening wolves." (Matt. 7:15, KJV)

The Devil: I planted you in his house for a reason, and that is to infiltrate and to orchestrate divisiveness. There's at least one of you located in every one of his houses, (church) disguised in each auxiliary. I need someone on the inside to ascertain their strength and weakness and to sow discord among his followers. Don't blow your cover under any circumstance! Be extremely discreet because his followers have the gift of discernment. They will immediately spot an imposter miles away.

Jesus: "Behold, I stand at the door and knock: If any man hear my voice, and open the door." (Rev. 3:20a, KJV)

The Devil: **No, no, no!** Let me interrupt! I don't have to knock. I know I'm always welcome and would just walk right on in. However, I will kick down the door if that option no longer exists.

Jesus: "I will come in to him, and will sup with him, and he with me." (Rev. 3:20b, KJV)

The Devil: I'm with you **24/7**. You don't need him to sup or share an evening meal. Besides, two's a company, three's a crowd, and I was here first.

Matthew: "The Son of man shall send forth his angels, and they shall gather out of his kingdom all things that offend, and them which do iniquity. And shall cast them into a furnace of fire: there shall be wailing and gnashing of teeth." (Matt. 13:41–42, KJV)

The Devil: He will certainly not do that. What loving father would torture his children by putting them in a burning furnace or lake of fire to burn eternally? I can truly say he loves his children too much to do such a terrible thing. Trust me, I know that for a fact from personal experience.

Jesus: "So then because thou art lukewarm, and neither cold or hot, I will spue thee out my mouth." (Rev. 3:16, KJV)

The Devil: Rejection, rejection, rejection! I will gladly accept all his rejects.

Jesus: "It is the spirit that quickeneth: the flesh profiteth nothing: the words that I speak unto you, they are spirit and they are life." (John 6:63, KJV)

The Devil: And full of contradictions.

Jesus: "Nevertheless I have somewhat against thee, because thou hast left thy first love." (Rev. 2:4, KJV)

The Devil: It sounds like he's jealous and wants you back. Don't make the same mistake twice. If you were satisfied with him, then you wouldn't have left him for me.

Jesus: "Then said Jesus unto his disciples, 'If any man will come after me, let him deny himself, and take up his cross, and follow me.'" (Matt. 16:24, KJV)

The Devil: It doesn't take all of that.

Jesus: "But you shall receive power, after that the Holy Ghost is come upon you, and you shall be witnesses unto me both in Jerusalem, and all Judea, and in Samaria, and the uttermost part of the earth." (Acts 1:8, KJV)

The Devil: Don't fret. You don't have to depend on his power because I have power also. Oh, by the way, I also have a whole lot more followers than he will ever have.

Paul: "That if thou shalt confess with thy mouth the Lord Jesus, and shalt believe in thine heart that God hath raised him from the dead, thou shalt be saved. For with the heart man believeth unto righteousness, and with the mouth confession is made unto salvation." (Rom. 10:9–10, KJV)

The Devil: Nonsense! Why can't he just accept you as you are?

John: "If you love me keep my commandments." (John 14:15, KJV)

The Devil: Too many ifs. He's yet not getting the message. Your action alone speaks loudly and clearly, telling him you no longer love him. What more can you do to get the message across? Nothing at all!

Peter: "Casting all your care upon him: for he careth for you." (1 Pet. 5:7, KJV)

The Devil: Haven't I proven to you that I care? Didn't I aid you in casting your cares and your problems on someone other than me for you to get some rest and peace of mind?

Isaiah: "Thou wilt keep him in perfect peace, whose mind is stayed on thee: because he trusted in thee." (Isa. 26:3, KJV)

The Devil: He has only one option for a "so-called" peace of mind. I have thousands of mind-altering gimmicks that will give you complete peace, and it comes without a price.

John: "I saw a new heaven and a new earth… And the building of the wall of it was of jasper: and the city was pure gold, like unto clear glass… And the twelve gates were twelve pearls: every several gates were of one pearl: and the street of the city was pure gold, as it were transparent glass." (Rev. 21:1a, 18, 21, KJV)

The Devil: Extreme over exaggeration or hyperbole! It's not all that great. I know because I once lived there. If it was all that, then

I, along with a third of the city's citizens, wouldn't have abruptly left.

David: "For his anger endureth but a moment: in his favor is life: weeping may endure for a night, but joy cometh in the morning." (Ps. 30:5, KJV)

The Devil: If he loved you like he said he did, then he wouldn't make you cry at all.

God: "For I am the Lord your God: ye shall therefore sanctify yourselves, and ye shall be holy: for I am holy: neither shall ye defile yourselves with any manner of creeping thing that creepeth upon the earth." (Lev. 11:44, KJV)

Paul: "According as he hath chosen us in him before the foundation of the world, that we should be holy and without blame before him in love." (Eph. 1:4, KJV)

The Devil: What's love got to do with such foolishness! *Living holy!* His expectation is **way too high!** You are only mere humans and will never reach that goal.

Luke: "And when he had spoken these things, while they beheld, he was taken up: and a **cloud** received him out of their sight." (Acts 1:9, KJV)

The Devil: How selfish. He was thinking only of himself by not allowing others to get on the cloud with him. Don't be dismayed, for there are spacious rooms yet available on my cloud, which is **cloud nine.** *There, you can do what you wanna do.* I put hundreds of thousands on it in which many are yet there, and enjoying every second of it.

Church Members: The devil is too cunning. The devil is destroying my life, my home, and my children. The devil is making it too hard for me to live a saved life. The devil won't leave me alone. The devil made me do it.

The Devil: Thank you so very much, nonetheless, pestering people is what I do best. That's my specialty, and I have mastered it.

However, I am so tired of all you church folks blaming me for every bad situation occurring in your lives as a result of your poor choices.

Jesus: "As the Father knoweth me, even so know I the Father: and I lay down my life for the sheep" (John 10:15, KJV). "And when they were come to the place, which is called Calvary, there they crucified him, and the malefactors, one on the right hand, and the other on the left. Then said Jesus, 'Father forgive them: for they know not what they do'" (Luke 23:33–34, KJV).

The Devil: OH NO, I CAN'T TOP THAT. THERE'S NO GREATER LOVE THAN THAT. I CAN'T COMPETE WITH A LOVE SUCH AS HIS. I BELIEVE EVERY WORD HE SAID, AND ALL I CAN DO IS TREMBLE. YOU'RE ON YOUR OWN. GOOD LUCK. YOU'RE GONNA NEED IT!

"And let the church say, 'Amen, Amen, Amen.'"

Food for Thought

---

1. *There are exceptions to every rule.*
2. When in doubt, think again before making the final decision, because in the moment of indecisiveness, there's a fifty percent chance of a negative outcome. Even so, praying for guidance is not a bad choice.
3. It's really not free advice if one is pressured or made to feel obligated to accept it. The free advice then becomes a requirement.
4. The road to success is measured not by when, where, how, or the time it took you to arrive. The fact you indeed arrived in spite of is all that matters.
5. Whenever you reach success, always remember you didn't get there on your own.
6. Never burn the bridge you crossed to succeed because that's the one that got you there.
7. It's better to be dirt-poor and happy than it is to be filthy rich and miserable.
8. There's nothing like the first. You cannot duplicate the first no matter how many times you try.
9. A first impression is not always impressive.
10. A first impression can lead to another rejection.
11. The first impression is a lasting expression. Therefore, make a good first impression. If not, then make a better last expression because it's the one that may stick. The last thing said or done is usually the last thing remembered.
12. You will never get a second chance to make a first impression, so make every attempt to get it right the first time.
13. The quality of benevolences given will have a far more lasting effect than the quantity given.

14. Stay calm and be alert when provoked because upset is nothing but a setup switched around in order to take you out of your character.
15. The three most expensive things that a person needs and most people can't afford to give, are not money or things. It is time, a listening ear, and themselves, which is the most precious treasure.
16. You can always find some good in everybody, if you look for it. Keep looking. There is a jewel buried beneath the rubbish.
17. For every action, there is a reaction, whether it be negative or positive. Being proactive, in most cases, will prevent negative reactions.
18. There's no problem with being angry. It's your belief about the event that causes the anger, and your response to the event is what can cause the problem. There are always two thoughts that enters the mind when one gets angry. The first thought is to even the score by any means necessary. The second thought is the voice of wisdom that reveals the consequences of your inappropriate action. Try your very best to wait on the second thought before taking action. It will never steer you wrong.
19. The most difficult person to examine is one's own self.
20. Stay alert! Your enemies can't do you great harm once you're able to identify who they are.
21. A day that goes by is a day that can never be retrieved. Be happy, and live each day to the fullest because, eventually, it will be your last.
22. It is impossible to make up for lost time. Lost time is never found.
23. Trying to make up for lost time only puts you further behind in the present time.
24. End each day with positive, uplifting words and actions. Don't let a new day catch you with old regrets.
25. It's the small things that make a big difference. One friendly smile can lift a hundred people's spirits in a matter of seconds. How important is a penny? If a person is one penny short of having a million dollars, are they a millionaire yet?

26. You cannot reason with an unreasonable person. So don't even try!

27. You never get too old for acquiring knowledge. If life's experience is the best teacher, then knowledge is the best student.

28. Books will tell you how things ought to be, while life teaches you how things really are.

29. Just because someone put you in a gutter, it doesn't mean you should wallow in it, because it doesn't mean you belong there. The same holds true if they put you on a pedestal. It doesn't mean you should take a seat, because you may not belong there either.

30. Take pride in whatever you do, no matter if the task is large or small. Anything worth doing is worth doing well, so do it well the first time or not at all.

31. If it's not your best, then don't continue the rest.

32. Staying active and vibrant prevents boredom, and being bored is boring.

33. For everything done under the sun, there is a season, and for everything that's not done that should have been done, there is a reason.

34. You can plan the event but not the outcome. Don't stress.

35. Surrounding yourself with positive people ensures positive results.

36. You can usually tell a person's character by who they hang out with. The same holds true, you can also pinpoint a person's character by the manner in which they treat their mom.

37. When you're sick and tired of being sick and tired, and tired of being tired and sick, then you just may be on the road to deliverance.

38. If your word is worth very little, then your promises are worth zilch. A promise is no more than a bunch of words tied together.

39. Don't be so quick to bail. Stay the course. Just as if you don't like what you see on the movie screen, you don't throw the projector away. You change the film instead. Sometimes it's the person themselves who needs to change their own views or thoughts before bailing out.

40. A person usually won't change unless they feel that what they're getting is greater than what they're giving up to get it.
41. A change will not occur unless there's something to compare the change to.
42. Changing the behavior is impossible without changing the thought process.
43. Never give anyone the permission to define you. You are a special person, and don't need any validations to confirm that fact.
44. You are who you say and think you are and not who others say or think you are. Let no one define who you are. Put your confidence in yourself and in your own abilities. The person that defines you is the one who will control you.
45. Truth, is it a perception or reality? One person's truth can be another person's perception.
46. Some people sadly confuse facts with perception and interpretation. Perception is the way things could be. Interpretation is the way things should be. Facts are the way things really are.

There are at least three times in a person's life that you should refrain from attempting to borrow money. They are: (1) When they are preparing for a vacation trip. (2) During the vacation trip. (3) When they return from the vacation trip. When someone is preparing for the vacation trip they are budgeting their money for the trip. During the vacation trip, they are spending their money, and when they return from the vacation trip, they are broke because they have spent all their money at the conclusion of the vacation trip.

Friendships

---

1. A friend is priceless. They are a gift from God and cannot be bribed or bought.

2. Some people come into your life for a season, there are others who come for a reason, but a friend will come into your life and stay forever.

3. What is it that set a **friend** and **true** friend apart? There is no difference between a friend and a true friend. A friend is true. However, there's a big difference between a friend and acquaintance.

4. How do one differentiate between a **friend** and **best** friend?

5. A friend will love you at all times.

6. It's a lot easier to count the number of friends than it is to count the number of acquaintances. If you are blessed to have at least one friend in your lifetime, then you've done well.

7. Need a friend? Be a friend.

8. Best way to eliminate your enemy is to win them over as a friend.

9. A friend will love you for eternity and will accept you just as you are.

10. It's best to have one friend than ten thousand acquaintances.

11. The depth of a friend can be measured by their presence during your times of adversities.

12. A friend is like a stain in a garment—no matter how many times you put them through the wringer, they will not disappear.

13. There are some people who are very difficult to love, and there are others who are nearly impossible to hate.

Brainwork

---

1. Law-abiding citizens are not always law abiding.
2. A person can be legally blind and have twenty-twenty vision, just as a person can have twenty-twenty vision and yet be blind. Sometimes good insight is better than good eyesight.
3. Some people mistake disabled for handicap. Handicap, in a lot of cases, is in the mind. It's mind over matter. As the old saying goes, "If you don't mind, then it doesn't matter." A person who can, but is unwilling to exercise their ability to overcome what appears to be insurmountable obstacles or challenges set before them, although being otherwise healthy, is mentally handicapped.
4. When asking for forgiveness or accepting an apology, never start a new sentence with "*But...*" such as "Please forgive me, *but...*" or "I accept your apology, *but...*" *Buts* take the strength away from the apology, as well as the request for forgiveness, and creates a new debate or ill feeling toward the parties involved.
5. Sometimes it is easier to forgive others who hurt you than it is to forgive yourself for hurting them.
6. Good intentions does not always ensure good results.
7. Bad deeds with good intentions can make a bad situation.
8. You will not know you've hit rock bottom 'til you land there.
9. Once you hit rock bottom, anything that occurs after that is progress.
10. It takes a strong, courageous man to walk away from a fight. Any coward will eventually fight if you push them long and hard enough.
11. It's best to have grandchildren before you have your own children, for it would better prepare you in raising your own children.

12. If you refuse to **sit** through the beginning, then you can easily **jump** to the conclusion, which is usually far from the truth.

13. First things first: be patient and take your time. You can't get to one million without getting to one. If it's meant for you to have, it will eventually get to you.

14. Obtaining and utilizing the triple *Cs*—**communication, compassion,** and **common sense**—is essential to surviving any relationship.

15. Common sense is a treasure. It is a good substitute for ignorance.

16. Common sense is not complicated. However, trying to differentiate between common sense and nonsense can be a tad bit confusing.

17. Common sense is not as widespread as it seems to be.

18. Most problems can be avoided by exercising common sense as opposed to intelligence.

19. It's not rationalizing or analyzing if it makes good sense.

20. Think twice, speak once. If people would only think before they say it, then they probably wouldn't say it.

21. The harder you try not to be like *that* person, the more you become *that* person, unless you break the cycle. Break the cycle, and start anew.

22. A lie will need a crutch or two to stand on, while the truth will stand firmly on its tippy toes.

23. A wise person will not attempt to feed their ego because they know it's greedy and will always want more.

24. For every loophole, there is a stronghold. And for every stronghold, there is a loophole. There's always a way out, hang in there, your breakthrough is nearer than you realize.

25. I only know what I know, and one thing I do know is that I got enough sense to know I don't know everything.

26. If you continue to think for a person, then you take away that person's ability to think for themselves. If a person who choose not to think for themselves, then they can't truly live. Thinking is the fuel that simulates the brain, and the body takes orders from the brain.

27. Lower my standards! It's perfectly OK to set high **standards**, however, it would be advantageous to lower the *expectation* of others meeting your set *standards*. It creates a balance, and could possibly prevent mental anguish from the parties involved.

Pessimist and Optimist

Don't be afraid of all the things that
could go wrong, instead be more excited
about all the things that can go right.
—*Imani Elizabeth Sampson*

1. A *pessimist* will complain that **twenty-four** hours is not enough time in a day to complete the tasks. An *optimist* will view it from a different perspective and say, after completing the many tasks set before them, "**One** day consists of **86,400** seconds, and now I have way too much time on my hands."

2. If you ask an *extreme pessimist* for **one hour** of their time, they would angrily respond, "What! That's **three thousand six hundred seconds**, you're being inconsiderate and ridiculous." A pessimist would respond, "That's **sixty minutes**," and complain that it would take too much of their precious time. An optimist would gladly say, "**Only one hour**? Sure, is that all the time you need?"

3. The best place to find the truth between two opposing views is in the middle. Every debater is right in their own eyes.

4. Communication involves listening and learning. You must first listen to learn, and once you learn, you then must learn to listen.

5. When giving constructive criticism or advice, always end it with a positive statement.

6. After all you're getting, get a good understanding. It could save a lot of heartaches and regrets.

7. "In any verbiage exchange, it's never about being right. It's always about understanding." **Jacoby Sampson**

8. Let all things be done in moderation. If once is more than enough, then twice is overkill.

9. Thrifty or Spendthrift? A wise man, or woman possessing a thousand dollars, will skillfully attempt to find a thousand ways to save it. On the contrary, a foolish man, or woman possessing a million dollars will lavishly create a million ways to spend it.

10. If you are walking and spot a penny lying on the ground or payment, would you ignore it, or pick it up? Why?

11. There's a thin line between unqualified and overqualified. They can both find you in the unemployment line.

12. Negativity leads to a dead-end situation, but there are many avenues that lead to positive results.

13. Opportunity knocks once, but failure will kick down the door.

14. No one is perfect, not even a perfectionist. There's always room for improvement.

15. You're not a failure 'til you say you are.

16. Dead minds exist due to buried emotions.

17. An individual who continues to fool other people makes them a fool. An individual who continues to fool himself makes themselves a bigger fool.

Maximize-Minimize

1. Maximizing your efforts will minimize your failures.
2. Maximizing fulfilling your dreams will minimize your nightmares.
3. Maximizing your opportunities will minimize regrets.
4. Maximizing positive thoughts will minimize negative results.
5. Maximizing forgiveness will minimize bondage.
6. Maximizing progression will minimize complacency.
7. Maximizing being open-minded will minimize isolation.
8. Maximizing cheers will minimize tears.
9. Maximizing happiness will minimize loneliness.
10. Favoritism ushers in ostracism.
11. Some people would rather change relationships than their mind, even when it's obvious they are wrong.
12. Some people would rather try to change the facts rather than their own opinions.
13. Some people would rather change doctors than their bad habits.
14. One of the greatest gifts that you can give yourself and others simultaneously is forgiveness. Forgiving someone who offended you free both of you from bondage. It frees the one who offended you from the bondage of guilt. It frees you from the bondage of bitterness or ill-feeling developed toward them.
15. Forgiving others is the necessary key in freeing oneself.
16. What you give a person may make a little difference, but what you show a person will make a larger impact (e.g., love, compassion, consideration, kindness, courtesy, empathy, and so forth).
17. The best-kept secret is the one that's kept.
18. A person who can't keep their word, cannot be trusted to hold your secrets or keep anything else.

19. A person who uses unhealthy substances as a means to cope or escape from unpleasant events, circumstances, or situations is in the same dangerous position as a healthy rat eating good cheese from a rat trap.

20. "Don't pretend. Be yourself. The thing is when you're two different people, one is bound to trip over the other." *Jacoby Sampson*

21. How important is laughter? Laughter is an antidote. It is to the soul, as medicine to the body. Take for instance, if two or more people are having a conflict. Take note, if someone makes a humorous comment, and one or all parties burst out in laughter, immediately, the highly tense emotions decrease. Although laughter does not resolve the problem, it does pave the way for better communication, and communicating is the best tool in resolving most conflicts.

22. The countenance of a person in their latter years may be determined by how they weathered the storms in their former years.

23. When life's burdens keep knocking you down, keep getting back up. Recognition is not given based on how many times you're knocked down but how many times you get up. Get up!

24. Everybody wins in a successful dialogue. However, in an unhealthy debate, no one wins. If one person thinks they won, then the perception is the other person lost. If so, that increases alienation between the parties involved. Therefore, everyone loses in an unhealthy debate. Always choose dialogues over debates. Working toward a common understanding or agreement should be the goal.

25. The most unlikely person to succeed is the one who is afraid to try.

26. Keep persevering. Success or failure does not occur overnight.

27. "Dreams without goals are just thoughts, and goals without steps are just ideas. Stay the course. Dreams minus efforts are just as worthless as a well laid out plan with no ambition to see it through." *Jacoby Sampson*

28. "Living your dream is better than chasing it, sit back, relax and enjoy the energy it gives you." *Jacoby Sampson*

29. If at first you don't succeed, learn from your mistake and try, try again.
30. Always choose carefully. Choices are optional. Consequences are mandatory.
31. It starts at the top. If you heal the father, then you will heal the son, and so on.
32. **Anything** that is required in order for one to be the recipient of a gift makes the gift no longer a gift but a purchase.
33. To honor one's parent, parents, or guardian, the child must be a PRO: **p**roductive, **r**espectful, and **o**bedient. And they must follow the good example set by their parent, parents, or guardian.
34. Never push your child to be the best in order to be successful. Instead, motivate them to be the best they can be. Reaching that goal in itself is a success.
35. When a child's grades drop, it could be a clear indication that the parenting skills grade dropped.
36. The law of greed or curiosity: a person who can have anything they want, usually want what they can't have.
37. Humility is when you know you're far ahead of the class but choose to sit in the back row, far away in the corner of the room, so that others to get an opportunity to shine.
38. A wise person will learn from their mistake and move forward. A foolish person will keep doing what they do and keep getting the same negative results, then blame others for it.
39. If you do not correct the mistake, you're bound to repeat it. The one thing that's worse than making a mistake is not learning from it.
40. Embrace adversities and obstacles for they are the tools for growth and building character when used properly.
41. A positive person does not see barriers and obstacles as a roadblock and retrieve but as a stepping stone and proceed.
42. "Leap for the sky. If you never leap, then you'll never know what's it's like to fly." *Jacoby Sampson*
43. If you can't see far, then you will not go far. Visualization plays a great role in one's determination, motivation, and finally their destination.

44. A soft answer is soothing words to a heated argument, and it takes away the strength from the wrath, just as a cool breeze on a hot day is more soothing than a strong wind on a warm day.
45. What do you give a person who has everything that money can buy? Give them everything money can't buy, such as, love, faithfulness, hope, compassion, peace, friendship, and so forth.

Love

1. Which would you prefer: to have loved and lost or to have never loved at all? Why?
2. Love is the miraculous power that compels one to do the unthinkable without giving it a second thought.
3. Love is emotions in progress.
4. Love is action. Love is not acting or reacting.
5. Good men become good friends, while bad men becomes boyfriends.
6. The most powerful forces in the world is **love**, **family**, **friends**, and, lastly, money.
7. If given the choice, would you rather be a fool in love, or be loved by a fool? Why, or why not?
8. It is better to be very poor and happy with someone who loves you than it is to be abundantly rich and miserable with someone who despises you.
9. Love is the surest foundation to build any relationship. Anything short of love can be compared to the Humpty Dumpty syndrome. "Humpty Dumpty sat on the wall, Humpty Dumpty had a great fall; all the king's horses and all the king's men, couldn't put Humpty together again." Additionally, if the foundation is not built on love, then the relationship will eventually come tumbling down, and nothing outside of love can put it back together again.
10. If it doesn't hurt, then, it's not love. It hurts to be in love. Isn't it strange how love feels so good, and yet hurts so bad? Is it worth it? Why or why not?
11. Love shines the brightest in your darkest hours.
12. There's a thin line between love and lust.
13. A Life-Changing Decision: Choose carefully. A man may hold the keys to his house, but a woman holds the key to his heart.

14. To be loved is one of a person's greatest desires.
15. Good looks are temporary, and it slowly fades away. Love is forever, contrary to what others may say.
16. Good looks get them into your house. Love and good personality gets them into your heart and keeps them there.
17. A nice body and good outer beauty will capture their attention, while good inward beauty captures their heart and soul.
18. In spite of all the riches that you have gained, even if you conquered the world, without love, you have nothing.
19. Which is more important in a marriage or relationship: love or sex? Why?
20. Women, don't allow them to sweep you off your feet if you cannot or are unwilling to trust them to carry you. And men, don't be so eager to sweep them off their feet if you're not willing to love, respect, provide, protect and to carry them throughout the duration.
21. The **two** saddest combinations of words in any language is "*Too late!*" and "*What if…*" is a close second.
22. The **three** most powerful combinations of words in any language is "*I love you.*"
23. It is better to grow into love as opposed to falling into it. Growing into love allows you to experience and enjoy the beauty of it before you arrive.
24. Everybody falls in love, but nobody falls out of love. Without the proper nourishment on a consistent basis, love will eventually die, and if that occurs, then it will be extremely difficult to bring it back.
25. Whether you grow into love or fall into love, be very sure you have a quick-mending heart because it will be broken many, many times. Eventually, it will mend every single time.
26. Permanent relationships breakups in many cases, are the result of temporarily unrepaired communication breakdowns.
27. Love does not keep count of the number of forgiveness.
28. You never forget your first love, no matter if it was a pleasant or unpleasant experience.

29. "I love you and give you my heart." Big mistake! Never give them your heart because if they leave, they will surely take it with them. Instead, give them all the love you have within your heart. If they decide to leave, they can only take the love you had for them. They can't take the love you'll have for the next person because it's not transferrable.

30. A wise person will never let go of a sure thing unless they are confident they have found something much better. In a lot of cases, that something much better is that which was rejected.

31. In all conflicts, work toward a common agreement, as opposed to winning. It's a sure way to prevent head-on collisions. There will be no head-on collision if you are all traveling in the same direction.

32. There's a huge difference between a wedding and a marriage. A wedding is the event (the sprint). A marriage is forever (the marathon).

33. If you treat her like your queen, then you will be her king forever.

34. If you allow him to be your king, then you will receive royal treatment forever.

35. Remember, she's your queen and not your maid.

36. Remember, he's your king and not your slave.

37. Nourishing a marriage or relationship allows it to blossom.

38. In a healthy relationship, both individuals must be willing to compromise. It should be give and take between both parties. No one demands to have their way only and not consider the other party's need.

39. Always respect and listen to another person's point of views and opinions, whether you agree or not. Listening is not a sign of agreeing, but it can be a tool of seeing it from a different perspective.

40. If you love someone, you will make every attempt to resolve the issues.

41. It takes two to build a marriage, but it only takes one to tear it down.

42. Be very sure you're completely healed from the previous painful relationship before you start a new one, lest you make the new person pay for the sins of the previous one.

43. You will not fall in love with the new person until the love from the previous relationship dies.

44. Also, a person will not fall in love with the new man or woman until the wound from the previous relationship becomes a scar. The scar is a clear indication that the wound has healed and serves as a reminder of the painful experience, and for you to avoid making the same or similar mistake again.

45. If someone loves at 99.9 percent, they are only giving a fraction of their love, and that's not good enough. Each party must be willing to do the whole hundred. Anything taken from the whole only weakens it.

46. **The love test** (hindsight): would you enter into the relationship with the individual you're with if you knew then what you know about them now? Why or why not?

47. If the person you're in love with is no longer in love with you, which is easier: to try to hold on or to let go? Why?

48. If a magnet ceases to attract other objects, is it still a magnet? If love ceases to draw others, is it still love? Why or why not?

49. It is easier to walk away from hatred than it is to walk away from love.

50. If you can explain love, then it's not love. Love is unexplainable. It certainly is describable.

51. A healthy fight (disagreement) in any relationship does not destroy it, but serves as a great tool to strengthen it.

52. Does he still make you laugh? Why or why not? Does she still make you laugh? Why or why not?

53. Together, together, together yet separated. It's always better to work it out together.

54. A unique relationship is where opposite attracts, being different yet one and the same.

55. It may be okay to talk about the terrible person you were as long as *that person* you were is not the identical person you are.

56. The best way to get even with the ones who rejected you is to move on in spite of, to succeed and be happy without them.

57. If someone knowingly hurt the ones they love without apologizing and afterward have a good night sleep, that love can and will be questioned.

58. "The moment their time becomes an option for you, then your presence will no longer be a priority for them." *Jacoby Sampson*

59. If you could only choose one, which would you prefer? Love and happiness or love and money? Why?

60. Sometimes it's better to repair a broken relationship than it is to attempt to replace it.

61. Love involves giving your all. However, just because one does not feel they are being loved by the other party it doesn't necessarily mean that love is not present. Just because blood is not getting to the brain it does not mean there is no blood in the body and the heart's not pumping the blood. There's something that's hindering the blood from flowing through the channels. Just as there may be something hindering the love from flowing through the love channels.

62. If you are not prepared to accept or live the rest of your life with them as they are, then don't marry them. Why mess up two lives?

63. It is a lot easier for a young woman to convince her boyfriend's mother that she's the right lady for her son than it is for a young man to convince his girlfriend's father that he's the right man for his daughter. To the father, his daughter will always be **daddy's little girl** no matter what age she may be, and no man is good enough for her. However, the father may be willing to make exceptions in some instances if the man can pass the fatherly test.

64. Loving others first begins with loving yourself.

65. Spend less time and energy on trying to get a person of low esteem to love you. Instead, spend more time and energy in teaching or encouraging them to love themselves. It's merely

impossible for a person to love others if they are unable to discover the love they have within themselves.

66. It was said that it only takes a minute to fall in love, but I say it could take a lifetime and a day to walk away from it.

67. Who's in charge? Are you in control of love, or are you controlled by love?

68. *Ladies*: Another feller is better—the one who will treat you like a queen—than another dude who acts like a fool, with a mind as if he was thirteen.

69. *Fellers:* Another lady is better—the one who is willing to be your queen—than the foolish woman who can't appreciate your kindness and your precious love doesn't mean a thing.

70. A foolish man will try to figure a woman out. A wise man understands that he cannot figure her out and leave it at that.

71. Open communication is the key to any successful relationship.

72. Everybody needs somebody sometimes. No one person has it all. It's not a curse. It's by design.

73. No one can survive on their own. Just as a puzzle is not complete until the last piece is connected firmly in its rightful place, neither are we until we are firmly connected to that special someone.

74. *Husband* to wife: "Sweetheart, *behind* every good man, there is a good woman."

Wife to husband: "No, honey. Don't you mean *beside* every good man, there is a very good woman?"

Husband to wife: "No, darling. Like I said, *behind* every good man there is a good woman." He added, "I would prefer you standing behind me to catch me when or if I fall."

Wife to husband: "My dear husband, that may be true, but if I walk by your side, then you would never fall. This I know because I won't let you."

The Difference Between Having Sex and Making Love

Is there a difference between having sex and making love? To some there are no differences, they are the same. And to others, it doesn't matter. Their only concern is about the thrill involving the act. I will explain the difference between having sex and making love. Albeit it, I'm not an expert in this matter, I'm far from it, but being married to my first love for fifty years gives me firsthand experience, which in my opinion is a good substitute for book knowledge.

Having sex is a physical act/experience or intimacy with no emotional connection. I have heard many men and women as well, boasting about how great or skillful they are in satisfying their mates. But between the sheets, if the intimacy is limited to having sex only, does it matter if you are a pro or not? Plus, if a person is as great as they say, there would be no need to say a word, it will speak for itself. And if so, then let others do the boasting. It does not take a rocket scientist to figure out how to have sex, nor does it take unique skills to perform the act. Even animals and other creatures engage in sexual intercourse, they can attest to when it comes to having sex only, any living creature can perform the act.

In order to make love, there first *must*, I repeat, *must* be love. In other words, there must be a love connection. Without love, these two words (making love and having sex) don't belong together and should go their separate way. It's merely impossible to make love without love being shared by the couple. Still, a lot of people that are in love make the mistake of thinking that the bedroom or other private locations are where love-making begins. On the contrary, making love does not start in the bedroom or anywhere else. Making love starts long before you reach the bedroom. Sound ridiculous, right? Let me elaborate further on this statement. Making love is giving her the assurance that she is your queen and the most important person in your life. She is to be treated with the utmost respect that she deserves.

Making love to her *inside* the bedroom involves the small things you do for her *outside* of the bedroom, such as: Occasionally giving her "*just because*" gifts, a greeting card or, something special for example. Perhaps a small or large gift to express your love to her and how you appreciate the loyal commitment. It's not the size or price of the gift, but the *love, thought and effort that was put into the gift*. Even so, giving yourself to her is preferred over any gift you give, no matter how expensive or beautiful it may be. She needs to know that she is needed. It is of the utmost importance that you resist the temptation to compare her flaws to your mother, sister/ sisters' strength and expertise. In doing so could prevent her from issuing a friendly reminder that you did not marry your mother, or your sisters. Her desire is to complete you, helping you to reach your goal. These small gestures should be given between specific days, i.e., Birthday, Christmas, Valentine's Day, and so on.

Making love to her inside the bedroom involves setting time exclusive for the two of you alone. Spending quality time with her is a confirmation you love being in her presence and that she is esteemed above all others. It's not so much the quantity of time she seeks, the quality time spent with her is most important and preferably. It does not necessarily mean the time spent together must be a romantic setting. It could be going to the movie theater, luncheon, or, dinner date, going for walks together, or just remaining secluded in your residence, just the two of you. Also, occasionally to change the pace it would be nice to get away for a few days.

Helping out with the household chores should not be out of the realm. As for me, I assist my wife with washing the dishes. I do it the old fashion way, which means I wash them by hand, and not with the aid of the dishwasher, even though we have a dishwasher. Also, I mop and vacuum the floors. Assisting with these and other household chores does not make me less than a man as some traditional men believe. They hold the belief passed down to them by society that household chores are a woman's duty.

Making love to her inside the bedroom involves listening to her outside of the bedroom. This is vital and highly recommended. There are times when she does not want or expect you to fix the situation, she only wants to vent and needs your listening ear. That's all! She must have the assurance that you truly care about her, and that she is special. It was said a woman does not want to make love unless she feels that she is loved. If she's having a bad day and wants to talk to someone, *let it be you.*

Now on the flip side of the coin. Making love to him inside the bedroom also involves the small things you do for him outside of the bedroom, such as: Giving him the assurance that he is your king and the most important person in your life. He too must be given the utmost respect in return.

It involves supporting his dreams by assisting in any way possible to ensure he succeeds. That means a lot to him. Occasionally getting him greeting cards or gifts for no reason other than, "*just because.*" Likewise, giving yourself to him is most important and is secondary to the kind deeds shown. The just because gifts should be given between the specific days, i.e. Birthday, Christmas, Valentine's Day, and so on. You should walk by his side and not over or *on his head* to have it your way, and disregarding his wishes.

Making love to him inside the bedroom involves refraining from being condescending, even though you may be more intelligent. It doesn't matter if you are the most intelligent because you see it as an asset to the union. Also, you understand your weakness is his strength and his weakness is your strength.

Making love to him inside the bedroom involves building him up and not tearing him down by bombarding him with criticism or comparing his shortcomings to your father or another man's skillful abilities. Perhaps, this would prevent him from making a good-humored, smart-alecky remarks such as, "You should have married your father, or the other man mentioned."

Making love to him inside the bedroom involves having the wisdom to know when to give him space when he feels the need to be alone. Please don't get upset when he detects the sense of urgency to the need to go to his "*man cave*" to try and figure things out. His man cave may not necessarily be a particular or favorite place. Sometimes his man cave is withdrawing into himself, giving the appearance of shutting down and shutting others out. His man cave could be in his vehicle while driving to various destinations, watching T.V., lying awake while you're asleep, and so on. Desperately, he is trying to come up with a workable plan.

It's not that he is being mean or rude, he is only reverting to to his upbringing. It was instilled into most men from their youth to fix things, situations, and problems. This also includes problems presented to him during the relationship. So what goes through his mind when he is faced with a problem and does not have the answer, or the tools to fix it? He would temporarily go into seclusion, (physical or mental) spending time alone in his man cave or whatever is convenient as long as he is alone.

It is very important that you do not perceive that you are being ignored doing this phase. Try your best to understand that his desire to be alone to ponder over, and over how to come up with a remedy to fix the problem. Questioning his commitment during these times only create added pressure, because he feels the need to solve the problem, but feeling being ignored makes him feel guilty of neglecting you, even though he knows it is far from the truth. Even so, out of consideration and respect he must keep you in the loop and communicate his unintentional withdrawal. In doing so will prevent the perception of feeling alienated, and will keep the doors open for mutual understanding.

He cannot fully rest until he comes up with a solution to the problem, or accepts the fact the problem is beyond his control, if that is indeed the case. The problem may or may not directly involve you. But if he has a problem, indirectly, it will affect you because you love him. He fully understand that you love him dearly and is more than willing to pitch in. He is well aware that you have been supportive to no end. Rest assure he loves you, but feel that it's his responsibility to ensure the household is running smoothly.

His one and only purpose is to protect you from the unnecessary stress of fixing things that are broken, even though you may be better at fixing some things. If he's having a bad day and wants to talk to someone, *let it be you.*

Making love inside the bedroom involves some or more of the listed suggestions which takes place outside of the bedroom. If you do these things, the intimacy of making love leads to the bedroom which is the final act. The complete love-making cycle (this includes the kind gestures done before the final act) is equivalent to a *happy ending to a great movie.*

CONTRASTS

Having sex is two separate people interacting and then it's done.

Making love is two *lovebirds* coming together and being united as one.

Having sex involves just reaching a climax, but eventually, that gets old.

Making love, is love penetrating the heart, and reaching deep into the soul.

Having sex is giving a small portion, until the very next call.

Making love knows no other way, except to give your best, in essence, give your all.

Having sex could be a spur of the moment, afterward, it's time to run.

Making love is forever, the result of the sweet things done.

Having sex is void of feelings, and can very well be an illusion.

Making love is genuine love and a foregone conclusion.

Having sex involves only the mind, and is repeated farther down the road.

Making love involves giving the essentials, the mind, body, and soul.

Having sex means merely seeking the thrill, and that can lead to an obsession.

Making love is two hearts uniting to strengthen the mighty strong connection.

Having sex can be a selfish act, only for the enjoyment of a few moments of pleasure.

Making love is a precious jewel, a pleasant experience, and a lasting treasure.

More Delicious Tidbits

1. Too much information can be just as frustrating and confusing as too little information.
2. It's a lot easier for one person to lead ten thousand people than it is for ten thousand people to lead one person.
3. Grouchy this morning? A person who woke up on the wrong side of the bed, in most cases is a good indicator it was their starting point.
4. I would rather get one rose while I'm yet alive than to be surrounded by a truckload of them when I'm in my grave.
5. One genuine pat on the back when a person is alive is better than a fake one-hour standing ovation when they're lying in their casket.
6. It is very risky to ask a child for their honest opinion. Their truth just may be your insult.
7. Try to minimize the need to apologize for causing heartaches because an apology is not an eraser. While the apologetic words may ease the tension, it will not erase the pain from the hurting words or actions that penetrated the heart.
8. A very good reason, in most cases, is nothing more than a very poor excuse.
9. Adversities to a stubborn heart is like a constant rain to a very dry ground. The more it comes, the softer it gets.
10. You should put no more time, effort, and energy in aiding someone in solving their problems than they are willing to put in.
11. Be patient. Rushing to be number one? "The first will be last, and the last will be first." Remember that when you're rushing to beat the crowd to be the first to get on the elevator. Think about it. The last one to get on will be the first one to get off. This could also apply to many other first you're rushing to get ahead of others in life.

12. The greater the agony, the sweeter the victory.

13. Don't ever give up! The closer you get to the finish line (your goals), the harder it will seem to get there. Giving up then is just as foolish as a person who swam three quarters across the lake. They got tired, then turned around and swam back to the starting point.

14. Don't envy the ones who seem to have everything that money can buy. Those same people are most likely envious of you because you possess everything money cannot buy and yet are content.

15. You are in control of your destiny. If you don't reach your desired goal, it ain't nobody's fault but your own. **Willie E. Manning**

16. A simple definition of *priority*: priority is whatever you do first.

17. To insist on having one's way is a sign of immaturity, while self-restraint is evidence of growth.

18. If you, for whatever reason, are not willing to share another person's pain, then they may not be willing to share your joy and gain.

19. Complacency and stagnation are not twins, but they are in the same family.

20. Complacency is the end result of motivation hanging out with procrastination too long.

21. The 99.9 percent truth is a 100 percent lie.

22. Always be honest, be honest always. A person of integrity may lie occasionally, but a liar will only tell the truth by mistake.

23. It's always more advantageous to face the naked truth head-on than to be dazzled by a wardrobe of lies.

24. Most tears are caused by a broken heart that can no longer mask the pain.

25. What you say can be viewed as perception. What you do will be known as facts.

26. *The joy of gaining a child cannot be compared to the sorrow of losing one.*

27. Sweet memories made can never be erased. They will forever be embedded in your heart.

28. Death is a part of life.

    A good relationship last forever. Even though death ends a life, it does not end a relationship. The sweet memories made will last a lifetime.

29. Sometimes you have to lose somebody or something you love for a season in order to gain something better for a lifetime.

30. The most important three minutes: It's always better and more powerful to give them the three-minute tribute when they are alive than when lying in their casket.

31. "Why is it that people get more praise and recognition when they become just a memory?" ***Corinthia Faye Sampson***

32. To gain something of great value, will cost something of even greater value to obtain it.

33. It takes many years to build a good reputation, but one bad choice can tear it all down in a matter of seconds.

34. You must wise up before you can rise up. Therefore, wise up and rise up.

35. Unset boundaries are an open invitation for certain disasters.

36. If I only knew, I would.............. (fill in the blanks).

37. Don't get alarmed when people say negative things about you. However, be overly concerned and correct yourself if what they are saying is true.

38. Males are born. Gentlemen are raised. You can certainly raise a boy, but it's merely impossible to raise a man.

39. Never strive to reach perfection. Instead, push yourself to full capacity because once you reach perfection, then you die. There was one ***perfect man*** who walked the earth, and guess what happened to him!

40. There are two seasons—a season for blessings and a season for lessons. Embrace them both. The lessons precede the blessings. Slow learner, slow blessings. Quick learner, quick blessings.

41. Don't put your confidence in your emotions because emotions come and go. Emotions are only a secondary response from previous occurrences.

42. A few moments of pleasure can sometimes lead to a lifetime of guilt—a very unequal tradeoff.

43. When it rains, it pours, but when it stops, you soar. There's always a bright side to every circumstance. Keep on pushing.

44. Be honest: there' a huge difference between giving the correct answer and giving the true answer.

45. An inappropriate behavior that is justified is a behavior that cannot be rectified.

46. If you want a job done well, then you must do it yourself. Howbeit, someone will come along and do it even better.

47. Good things come to those who wait. Grab it quickly when it arrives, lest it quickly fades away.

48. "Crying time: it's okay to cry. Sometimes our tears are our strength." *Jacoby Sampson*

49. There is no fault or mistake so great that love cannot erase.

50. Don't get angry if someone is not clear on what you're conveying. It doesn't mean you're not expressing it clearly, nor is it an indication the other party or parties is slow or illiterate. It simply means that communication between you and the other party must continue.

51. Some blessings do not come without obstacles.

52. Be thankful: whatever you gained in this world is a blessing from God and not a reward.

53. Would you rather have a large amount of money for a short while or a small amount for a long time? Why?

54. There's a big difference between growing up and growing old. Growing old is about numbers. Growing up is more about maturity. Growing old is reaching a certain age. Growing up is reaching levels of maturity. Growing old is beyond one's control. Growing up is within one's full control.

55. One of the most painful and helpless feelings is being in the presence of someone you love who is suffering, and other than praying, there's not a thing you can do to alleviate the pain.

56. The only person who can't be fixed is the person who fails to realize that they are broken.

Red Flags

---

1. When they are more attracted to your body than your brain and inner beauty, or when your inward beauty is secondary to your outward beauty to them.
2. When the patterns change. Beware! When a person change their pattern, that's a good indication that something has changed. Patterns and fingerprints are alike in two aspects: (1) They never lie and (2) they both are consistent.
3. When they say all the wrong things.
4. When they say all the right things.
5. When you're no longer the first option.
6. If something seems too good to be true, proceed with caution because it usually is.
7. When they begin to pay more attention to your underage child/children than they do you.
8. When he is physical or verbal abusive to his teenage daughter/ stepdaughter for having sexual intercourse.
9. Gradual or abrupt withdrawal or isolation.
10. Be aware if one sees you in dire need and have the resources to assist you but say, "Let me know if you need anything." Word of advice: if they feel the need to offer aid instead of providing it, then they really don't want to do it.
11. When they no longer care about what you do, whether it is good or bad.
12. When they say it's free, with no strings attached. Sometimes in the long run, the free stuff comes with the most expensive attachments.
13. Be careful of the person with many words because if what they're offering is genuine, then it would speak for itself.
14. When someone says, "You don't owe me anything," for the kind deed(s) provided while simultaneously reaching for the

money you're holding in your hand that was offered, give them the money to prevent any possible ill feelings from them.

15. Frequent turnovers or changes.
16. If the person is not willing to put it in writing.

Perfect Peace

———————————

When we keep our minds on God, God gives
us peace of mind. For he promised to keep us
in perfect peace whose mind is stayed on him.
—*Joyce Ann Hanspard-Hewitt*

The simple direction to heaven: Turn **right**
and continue to go **straight** ahead.
Jesus loves us and it ain't nothing we can do about it.

Humorous

---

1. While the two were walking down the street on a dark, cloudy day, the man said to his friend, "I understand the weather forecast said we will get rain today, and I see you have two umbrellas. I can understand you having one to protect yourself from the rain." He then added, "But I don't understand why two umbrellas?"

    His friend's response was, "Yes, I have two umbrellas. The first umbrella is to protect myself from the rain, and I'm carrying the second one just in case it rains twice." ***Bobby W. Outley***

    Similar to the man's burden of carrying two umbrellas, sometimes we carry unnecessary baggage that can weigh us down, impede or prevent progress. These include: fears, worries, anxiety, resentments, unforgiveness and the like.

2. An inmate's response to a correctional officer after being disrespected condescendingly, "Why are you treating me as if you're are superior to me? Are you on a very long ego trip?" He added, "You are required to return to this same prison from eight to ten hours a day, five days a week or more. From where I sit, we both are doing time." The inmate went on to say, "You are told when to come and when to go." He added, "If you need to get permission to have lunch, take a break, when you can go home, and so forth. To ensure I stay behind bars, you must stay behind bars with me. The way I see it, we are in the same boat. In some way, we are both inmates. The small difference is I'm full-time, and you're part-time."

3. It was said that he who laughs last, laugh the longest, meaning a person can be successful in the end even though it initially appeared that they would not succeed. Or when ridiculed, you will have the last laugh in the end. But I will add, "He who laughs last doesn't understand the joke."

4. Want to stay a day ahead of the game? Then purchase the Sunday newspaper on Saturday.
5. "I'm going to be late for my own funeral!" you said. But I say, the only time a person is late for their own funeral or anything else is when they doesn't show up.
6. An old Southern saying is that, "If it thunders before sevein (7 a.m.), it's gone rain before leven (11 a.m.)." They were pretty accurate in their prediction. In other words, take heed. The warning precedes the catastrophe.
7. Why beat a dead horse (complaining about the same thing over and over again)? When the horse dies, get off, and get on another one. In essence, let the past go and move on.
8. What do you call a person who possesses a wealth of knowledge and intelligence?
    Answer: A brilliantnaire ($$$$$$$$)
9. It was once said, "If you don't like my apples, then don't eat off my tree," meaning if you don't like the person or their ways, then cut ties. But I say, if you don't like another person's apples, then plant your own tree, or work on yourself and don't point fingers and criticize others as long as you have flaws. Also, if you can't appreciate another person's way of doing things, then try to create your own path.
10. A wife asked her husband why he refuses to renew their wedding vows. His humorous reply was, "Honey, the reason I don't want to renew our vows are that I make every effort to avoid making the same mistake twice." Nevertheless, he happily agreed to renew their vows. *Lee Sampson*
11. It was said *back in the day*, "If you give a man enough rope, he will hang himself."
    But I say in this day, "If you give him enough rope, he will hang you instead."
12. "Give the devil an inch, and he will take a mile." Give him a millimeter, and he will take your life.
13. Mom said to her children as she read from the Bible, "In the book of Job, it says that Job was tested by God. Job was a rich man, and God allowed Satan to destroy his cattle, servants, and

his riches." The Mother then added, "Finally, all of Job's children were killed." She then looked at her children and said, "I admire Job's patience and faith." She went on to say, "I would like to be like Job."

Her children responded in unison, "Mom, are you really saying you want us dead?"

14. A man went to see his physician regarding not being able to get an erection during the time of intimacy. After the physician examined him, he looked into the man's eyes and told him that he had been diagnosed with erectile dysfunction. The man didn't understand what it all meant but was reluctant to ask the doctor for clarification in fear of being perceived as a "dummy."

So he returned home and approached his wife with a confused and sad facial expression. His wife observed him struggling to find the right words to say, so before he began to speak, she asked him what did the doctor say was wrong. "Are you all right?" she anxiously asked.

The man mumbled, "I have terrible news. All hope is gone." His wife asked why he said such a thing, and his response was, "I say this because the doctor said when it comes to my manhood, my sexual *functioning* is no better than that of a *reptile*."

His wife immediately went into shock after hearing the devastating news. Gross miscommunication. If you don't know, ask more questions. The only dumb question is the question that is not asked.

15. Joe, is a middle age married man who was struck with a double whammy. He had very low Libido, extremely low testosterone and even a lower sex drive due his medical situation. One day he went to see his physician for a quick fix. Joe said, "Doc, can I get a prescription for Viagra?"

His physician responded, "Sure, Joe. How many did you want?"

Joe said, "It's quite simple Doc. One would be just fine."

His physician said, "Joe, why just one? I can surely give you more."

Joe said, "Thanks, Doc, but one will do. You see, I only need the Viagra for one night of pleasure, and for the next 364 days, I just need an excuse."

16. It was said that money can't buy love, but I say it sure can make a great down payment.

17. It was said that money isn't everything, but I say it's far ahead of what's ever in third place.

18. A wealthy man in his quest to capture a beautiful woman's heart said to her, "I will take you to any part of the world you would like to travel." He added, "And if that's not good enough, I will give you everything your precious little heart desire."

The woman responded without hesitation, "Sorry, but you can't buy me with your money or things. I'm not for sale." She so adamantly went on to say, "I have integrity, very high morals, and standards." She then paused briefly to think over the offer and quickly said, "Although you can't buy me with money or things, I'm not opposed to leasing."

19. How many miles does it take to run a 17.75-mile race?

Answer: 17.75. However, the minutes it take to run it will vary.

20. What was the exact time you fell asleep last night? Some things you will never know, so don't sweat the small details.

21. What is the surest way of separating yourself from an irresponsible acquaintance?

Answer: Loan them money!

22. Be very careful when loaning money to some people because when you loan them money, you contribute to freezing their memory bank.

23. If something or someone becomes impure, could it ever return to its purity state? Why or why not?

24. What do you say to someone who was fired from a good-paying job for continuing to take extended lunch breaks without permission?

Answer: "You swallowed a golden opportunity."

25. Does a 300 watt light bulb shine brighter at midday or midnight?

    Answer: No it does not. A 300 watt light bulb produce the same amount of energy (brightness) regardless. Even so, the brightness from the bulb is more noticeable at midnight than it is at midday.

26. A woman was in such an unbelievable reverse denial state and was dead set against childbearing, when her doctor gave the surprising news she was two months pregnant, her immediate response was, "It ain't mine!"

27. Good news, bad news, good news. The good news is there's **no** bad news. The bad news is there's no good news. There are times when no news is good news. In any case, be thankful because the news and situations could always be worse. As bad as your situation seems to be, there is someone who wishes they were in your shoes.

28. A short lesson on mutual respect. "My husband is the **head** in this household," said his wife. However, I am the **neck**, the head and the neck are connected. She said, "Therefore, you cannot circumvent the neck (myself) to get to the head (my husband) and vice versa. She went on to say, "The head and the neck are firmly connected together. Separately we will not survive."

29. A man informed his friend that he was going to a yard sale to make a purchase. "Yard sale!" the friend yelled. "Why would someone sell their yard?" *VSL* (very slow learner)!

30. If an irresistible force and an unmovable object collide, who wins? Explain your answer.

31. "If you can't stand the heat, then get out of the kitchen!" It mean to: stop complaining about difficult issues, or if you can't handle the truth or pressure, then remove yourself from the situation and let someone else do it. But I say absolutely not. If the heat gets too hot in the kitchen, then turn on the air conditioner which in essence is another way of saying, "Make the necessary adjustments based on the situation."

Absorption

---

1. The man said to the woman during the moment of passion, "I'm gonna play like a vampire and suck your neck."

   The woman replied, "If you do, and since we're playing, I'm gonna play like a priest and give you a *right* cross."

2. It has been said that it is rude to ask a woman her age, unless of course she looks a lot younger than her actual age. In that case, she may get offended if you don't ask her age.

3. Said the blind man to the woman who was trying to pull a fast one on him, "I may be blind, but I'm a long way from being in the dark."

4. Why wouldn't a completely satisfied person accept a million dollars that were offered to them with no strings attached?

   Answer: Because they're satisfied

5. The patient asks the dentist after getting a tooth pulled, "Doctor, did you get it all?"

   The dentist replied, "Yes, I did. I got the tooth, the whole tooth, nothing but the tooth.

6. Why do they call it restroom when it's the most inconvenient room to rest?

7. Why is it that when everything possibly goes wrong, it's at the worse time possible time every time?

8. Have you noticed that every time someone loses weight, your body mysteriously finds it? And every time you attempt to lose weight, there are no takers?

Patience is a Virtue

Be patient because time takes time.

One day, a little boy overheard his parents talking about the importance of patience and when used properly can be very beneficial to anyone, no matter the age, young or old. The little boy quickly got dressed, jumped on his bike, and rode to the nearby corner store to make a purchase. He walked up to the counter, reached into his pocket, and pulled out a balled-up, crumpled one-dollar bill, and handed it to the clerk. He politely said, "Sir, I wanna buy some patience."

The clerk took the crumpled dollar bill from the little boy's hand and pointed to a chair in the corner of the store. He said in a rude voice, "Go take a seat!"

The little boy smiled and said, "Yes, sir."

After taking a seat he reached into his pocket, pulled out a small toy, in a nonchalant manner began to play with it while the clerk assisted many customers who came after him.

After several hours had passed, when there were no more customers in the store, the little boy gleefully walked back up to the counter anxiously expecting to receive the patience he purchased hours ago. He was very polite and asked, "Sir, can I now have my patience?"

The clerk smiled while shaking his head in amusement. He said, "Son, you cannot buy patience with money or any such thing. It is earned by using self-discipline and not complaining or being rude when things are not going as you think they should." Also, the clerk said, "Son, you had patience when you walked through the door. However, you gained even more since you've been here." The clerk then reached into the cash register and pulled out the crumpled one-dollar bill, gently handed it to the little boy, along with a crisp five dollar bill.

The boy humbly replied, "Thank you sir, but I only gave you a dollar."

The clerk responded in a friendly voice, "I know you only gave me a dollar, son. Although it may not always come in money, patience is a virtue and has its rewards. One would need patience to succeed in this life." He added, "Son, you taught me a valuable lesson today. Please take the five dollar bill and come again. It is a pleasure having you as a customer."

Miscellaneous Proverbs

Dealing with Practical Situations

Deliberate Procrastination

"Don't withhold repayment of your debts. Don't say 'some other time,' if you can pay now." (Prov. 3:27–28, TLB)

Planning Ahead

"Take a lesson from the ants, you lazy fellow. Learn from their ways and be wise! For though they have no king to make them work, yet they labor hard all summer, gathering food for the winter. But you—all you do is sleep. When will you wake up? 'Let me sleep a little longer!' Sure, just a little more! And as you sleep, poverty creeps upon you like a robber and destroys you; want attacks you in full armor." (Prov. 6:6–11, TLB)

Taboo

"For there are six things the Lord hates— no, seven: haughtiness, lying, murdering, plotting evil, eagerness to do wrong, a false witness, sowing discord among brothers." (Prov. 6:16–19, TLB)

No Big Deal

"Hatred stirs old quarrels, but love overlooks insults." (Prov. 10:12, TLB)

Listen

"Don't talk so much. You keep putting your foot in your mouth. Be sensible and turn off the flow! When a good man speaks, he is worth listening to, but the words of fools are a dime a dozen." (Prov. 10:19–20, TLB)

His Blessing is Enough

"The Lord's blessing is our greatest wealth. All our work adds nothing to it!" (Prov. 10:22, TLB)

The Secret to Longevity

"Reverence for God adds hours to each day: so how can the wicked expect a long, good life?" (Prov. 10:27, TLB)

Fool's Gold

"Your riches won't help you on Judgment Day; only righteousness counts then." (Prov. 11:4, TLB)

More Than Good Looks

"A beautiful woman lacking discretion and modesty is like a fine gold ring in a pig's snout. The good man can look forward to happiness, while the wicked can expect only wrath. It is possible to give away and become richer! It is also possible to hold on too tightly and lose everything. Yes, the liberal man shall be rich! By watering others, he waters himself." (Prov. 11:22–25, TLB)

Putting the Cart Before the Horse

"To learn, you must want to be taught. To refuse reproof is stupid." (Prov. 12:1, TLB)

Her Excellence—His Joy

"A worthy wife is her husband's joy and crown; the other kind corrodes his strength and tears down everything he does." (Prov. 12:4, TLB)

Too Proud to Lift a Finger

"It is better to get your hands dirty—and eat, than to be too proud to work—and starve." (Prov. 12:9, TLB)

Be Cool

"A fool is quick-tempered; a wise man stays cool when insulted." (Prov. 12:16, TLB)

Pretense

"Deceit fills hearts that are plotting for evil; joy fills hearts that are planning for good!" (Prov. 12:20, TLB)

Thinking Ahead

"A wise man thinks ahead; a fool doesn't and even brags about it!" (Prov. 13:16, TLB)

Sidekicks

"Be with wise men and become wise. Be with evil men and become evil." (Prov. 13:20, TLB)

Stored Wealth

"When a good man dies, he leaves and inheritance to his grandchildren; But when a sinner dies, his wealth is stored up for the godly." (Prov. 13:22, TLB)

Necessity

"The good man eats to live, while the evil man lives to eat." (Prov. 13:25, TLB)

Self Destruction

"A wise woman builds her house, while a foolish woman tears hers down by her own efforts." (Prov. 14:1, TLB)

Avoidance

"If you are looking for advice, stay away from fools." (Prov. 14:7, TLB)

It Seems to be Right

"Before every man there lies a wide and pleasant road that seems right but ends in death." (Prov. 14:12, TLB)

Seeing is Believing

"Only a simpleton believes everything he's told. A prudent man understands the need for proof." (Prov. 14:15, TLB)

Insulting God

"Anyone who oppresses the poor is insulting God who made them. To help the poor is to honor God." (Prov. 14:31, TLB)

Under Construction

"Godliness exalts a nation, but sin is a reproach to any people." (Prov. 14:34, TLB)

Adding Fuel to the Fire

"A gentle answer turns away wrath, but harsh words cause quarrels." (Prov. 15:1, TLB)

Countenance Does Not Lie

"A happy face means a glad heart; a sad face means a breaking heart." (Prov. 15:13, TLB)

A Little Reverence is Best

"Better a little with reverence for God than great treasure and trouble with it." (Prov. 15:16, TLB)

Hidden Hatred

"It is better to eat soup with someone you love than steak with someone you hate." (Prov. 15:17, TLB)

Peacemaker

"A quick-tempered man starts fights; a cool-tempered man tries to stop them." (Prov. 15:18, TLB)

Choices

"A sensible son gladdens his father. A rebellious son saddens his mother." (Prov. 15:20, TLB)

No Filter

"A good man thinks before he speaks; the evil man pours out his evil words without a thought." (Prov. 15:28, TLB)

The Hall of Fame

"If you profit from constructive criticism you will be elected to the wise men's hall of fame. But to reject criticism is to harm yourself and your own best interests." (Prov. 15:31–32, TLB)

The Final Say

"We can always 'prove' that we are right, but is the Lord convinced?" (Prov. 16:2, TLB)

Forced Peace

"When a man is trying to please God, God makes even his worst enemies to be at peace with him." (Prov. 16:7, TLB)

Honesty is Better

"A little gained honestly is better than great wealth gotten by dishonest means." (Prov. 16:8, TLB)

Before and After

"Pride goes before destruction and haughtiness before a fall." (Prov. 16:18, TLB)

Stability in Humility

"Better poor and humble than proud and rich." (Prov. 16:19, TLB)

Yummy, Yummy, Yummy!

"Kind words are like honey—enjoyable and healthful." (Prov. 16:24, TLB)

Dead End

"Before every man there lies a wide and pleasant road he thinks is right, but it ends in death." (Prov. 16:25, TLB)

Motivation

"Hunger is good—if it makes you work to satisfy it!" (Prov. 16:26, TLB)

Idleness

"Idle hands are the devil's workshop; idle lips are his mouthpiece." (Prov. 16:27, TLB)

Bad Seeds

"An evil man sows strife; gossips separates the best of friends." (Prov. 16:28, TLB)

Wear Your "Crown" With Pride

"White hair is a crown of glory and is seen most among the godly." (Prov. 16:31, TLB)

Moderation

"It is better to be slow-tempered than famous; it is better to have self-control than to control an army." (Prov. 16:32, TLB)

Roll the Dice

"We toss the coin, but it is the Lord who controls its decision." (Prov. 16:33, TLB)

Choosing the Crust Over Steak

"A dry crust eaten in peace is better than steak every day along with argument and strife." (Prov. 17:1, TLB)

The Heart Purifier

"Silver and gold are purified by fire, but God purifies hearts." (Prov. 17:3, TLB)

Prevention

"It is hard to stop a quarrel once it starts, so don't let it begin." (Prov. 17:14, TLB)

Loyalty Forever

"A true friend is always loyal, and a brother is born to help in time of need." (Prov. 17:17, TLB)

Sign on the Dotted Line?

"It is poor judgment to countersign another's note, to become responsible for his debts." (Prov. 17:18, TLB)

Happy Heart—Happy Life

"A cheerful heart does good like medicine, but a broken spirit makes one sick." (Prov. 17:22, TLB)

Shush!

"The man of few words and settled mind is wise; therefore, even a fool is thought to be wise when he is silent. It pays him to keep his mouth shut." (Prov. 17:27–28, TLB)

It Doesn't Matter

"A rebel doesn't care about the facts. All he wants to do is yell." (Prov. 18:2, TLB)

A Lazy Man

"A lazy man is brother to the saboteur." (Prov. 18:9, TLB)

The Consequences of Pride

"Pride ends in destruction; humility ends in honor." (Prov. 18:12, TLB)

Check it Out

"What a shame—yes, how stupid!—to decide before knowing the facts!" (Prov. 18:13, TLB)

Always Open

"The intelligent man is always open to new ideas. In fact, he looks for them." (Prov. 18:15, TLB)

Generosity

"A gift does wonders; it will bring you before men of importance!" (Prov. 18:16, TLB)

The Complete Story

"Any story sounds true until someone tells the other side and sets the record straight." (Prov. 18:17, TLB)

Slow Down

"Those who love to talk will suffer the consequences. Men have died for saying the wrong thing!" (Prov. 18:21, TLB)

Soulmate

"The man who finds a wife finds a good thing. She is a blessing to him from the Lord." (Prov. 18:22, TLB)

Pretenders

"There are 'friends' who pretend to be friends, but there is a friend who sticks closer than a brother." (Prov. 18:24, TLB)

Blown Opportunity

"A man may ruin his chances by his own foolishness and then blame it on the Lord!" (Prov. 19:3, TLB)

Over Looked—Under Appreciated

"A wealthy man has many friends; the poor man has none left." (Prov. 19:4, TLB)

Generous Man—Many So-Called, Friends

"Many beg favors from a man who is generous; everyone is his friend!" (Prov. 19:6, TLB)

Compound Interest

"When you help the poor you are lending to the Lord—and he pays wonderful interest on your loan!" (Prov. 19:17, TLB)

Stand Down

"A short-tempered man must bear his own penalty; you can't do much to help him. If you try once, you must try a dozen times!" (Prov. 19:19, TLB)

From the Inside Out

"Kindness makes a man attractive. And it is better to be poor than dishonest." (Prov. 19:22, TLB)

I Need Help!

"Some men are so lazy they won't even feed themselves!" (Prov. 19:24, TLB)

Lesson Learned

"Punish a mocker and others will learn from his example. Reprove a wise man and he will be the wiser." (Prov. 19:25, TLB)

It's A Shame!

"A son who mistreats his father or mother is a public disgrace." (Prov. 19:26, TLB)

Enough

"Stop listening to teaching that contradicts what you know is right." (Prov. 19:27, TLB)

False Courage

"Wine gives false courage; hard liquor leads to brawls; what fools men are to let it master them, making them reel drunkenly down the street!" (Prov. 20:1, TLB)

I'll Pass

"It is an honor for a man to stay out of a fight. Only fools insist on quarreling." (Prov. 20:3, TLB)

Harvest

"If you won't plow in the cold, you won't eat at the harvest." (Prov. 20:4, TLB)

Say What?

"Most people will tell you what loyal friends they are, but are they telling the truth?" (Prov. 20:6, TLB)

I've Got A Secret

"Don't tell your secrets to a gossip unless you want them broadcast to the world." (Prov. 20:19, TLB)

Goodnight!

"God puts out the light of the man who curses his father or mother." (Prov. 20:20, TLB)

Ordered Footsteps

"Since the Lord is directing our steps, why try to understand everything that happens along the way?" (Prov. 20:24, TLB)

Count Up the Cost

"It is foolish and rash to make a promise to the Lord before counting the cost." (Prov. 20:25, TLB)

Justification

"We can justify our every deed, but God looks at our motives." (Prov. 21:2, TLB)

A Nagging Woman

"It is better to live in the corner of an attic than with a crabby woman in a lovely home." (Prov. 21:9, TLB)

Great Desires—No Efforts

"The lazy man longs for many things, but his hands refuse to work. He is greedy to get, while the godly love to give!" (Prov. 21:25–26, TLB)

Make the Right Choice

"If you must choose, take a good name rather than great riches; for to be held in loving esteem is better than silver and gold." (Prov. 22:1, TLB)

The Right Approach

"Teach a child to choose the right path, and when he is older, he will remain upon it." (Prov. 22:6, TLB)

"I Can't, I Can't, I Can't!"

"The lazy man is full of excuses. 'I can't go to work!' he says. 'If I go outside, I might meet a lion in the street and be killed!'" (Prov. 22:13, TLB)

Chastisement

"A youngster's heart is filled with rebellion, but punishment will drive it out of him." (Prov. 22:15, TLB)

Don't Do It!

"Unless you have the extra cash on hand, don't countersign a note. Why risk everything you own? They'll even take your bed!" (Prov. 22:26–27, TLB)

Bad Company

"Don't associate with evil men; don't long for their favors and gifts. Their kindness is a trick; they want to use you as their pawn. The delicious food they serve will turn sour in your stomach, and you will vomit it and have to take back your words of appreciation for their 'kindness.'" (Prov. 23:6–8, TLB)

Room for Growth

"Don't refuse to accept criticism; get all the help you can." (Prov. 23:12, TLB)

Mistakes Corrected

"Don't fail to correct your children; discipline won't hurt them! They won't die if you use a stick on them! Punishment will keep them out of hell." (Prov. 23:13–14, TLB)

It's All the Same

"To plan evil is as wrong as doing it." (Prov. 24:8, TLB)

Leave Him Alone!

"O evil man, leave the upright man alone, and quit trying to cheat him out of his rights. Don't you know that this good man, though you trip him up seven times, will each time rise again? But one calamity is enough to lay you low." (Prov. 24:15–16, TLB)

Timing is Everything

"Timely advice is as lovely as gold apples in a silver basket." (Prov. 25:11, TLB)

No Longer Welcome

"Don't visit your neighbor too often, or you will outwear your welcome!" (Prov. 25:17, TLB)

At Your Own Risk

"Putting confidence in an unreliable man is like chewing with a sore tooth, or trying to run on a broken foot." (Prov. 25:19, TLB)

One Thing Worse

"There is one thing worse than a fool, and that is a man who is conceited." (Prov. 26:12, TLB)

Stuck to the Bed

"The lazy man won't go out and work. 'There might be a lion outside!' he says. He sticks to his bed like a door to its hinges! He is too tired even to lift his food from his plate to his mouth! Yet in his own opinion he is smarter than seven wise men." (Prov. 26:13–16, TLB)

Mind Your Own Business

"Yanking a dog's ears is no more foolish than interfering in an argument that isn't any of your business." (Prov. 26:17, TLB)

Now You See it, Now You Don't

"Fire goes out for the lack of fuel, and tensions disappear when gossip stops." (Prov. 26:20, TLB)

Time Will Tell

"A man with hate in his heart may sound pleasant enough, but don't believe him; for he is cursing you in his heart, though he pretends to be so kind, his hatred will finally come to light for all to see." (Prov. 26:24–26, TLB)

Boomerang

"The man who sets a trap for others will get caught in it himself. Roll a boulder down on someone, and it will roll back and crush you." (Prov. 26:27, TLB)

Wait

"Don't brag about your plans for tomorrow—wait and see what happens." (Prov. 27:1, TLB)

It's Not Your Call

"Don't praise yourself; let others do it!" (Prov. 27:2, TLB)

Transparency

"Open rebuke is better than hidden love!" (Prov. 27:5, TLB)

Wounds are Better Than Kisses

"Wounds from a friend are better than kisses from an enemy!" (Prov. 27:6, TLB)

Tested and Proven

"Never abandon a friend—either yours or your father's. Then you won't need to go to a distant relative for help in your time of need." (Prov. 27:10, TLB)

Cantankerous Woman

"A constant dripping on a rainy day and a cranky woman are much alike! You can no more stop her complaints than you can stop the wind or hold onto anything with greasy hands." (Prov. 27:15–16, TLB)

Mirror, Mirror On the Wall

"A mirror reflects a man's face, but what he is really like is shown by the kind of friends he chooses." (Prov. 27:19, TLB)

No Satisfaction

"Ambition and death are alike in this: neither is ever satisfied." (Prov. 27:20, TLB)

Obey the Law

"To complain about the law is to praise the wickedness. To obey the law is to fight evil." (Prov. 28:4, TLB)

Succeeding the Right Way

"When the godly are successful, everyone is glad. When the wicked succeed, everyone is sad." (Prov. 28:12, TLB)

Grind

"Hard work brings prosperity; playing around brings poverty." (Prov. 28:19, TLB)

Get Rich Quick-Then, Quickly Disappears

"The man who wants to do right will get rich reward. But the man who wants to get rich quick will quickly fail." (Prov. 28:20, TLB)

Selling Out for Far Less

"Giving preferred treatment to rich people is a clear case of selling one's soul for a piece of bread." (Prov. 28:21, TLB)

Inflated Ego

"In the end, people appreciate frankness more than flattery." (Prov. 28:23, TLB)

Power in the Hands of the Wicked

"With good men in authority, the people rejoices; but with the wicked in power, they groan." (Prov. 29:2, TLB)

A Painful Lesson

"Scolding and spanking a child helps him to learn. Left to himself, he brings shame to his mother." (Prov. 29:15, TLB)

Only Two Favors

"O God, I beg two favors from you before I die: First, help me never to tell a lie. Second give me neither poverty nor riches! Give me just enough to satisfy my needs! For if I grow rich, I may become content without God. And if I am too poor, I may steal, and thus insult God's holy name." (Prov. 30:7–9, TLB)

More Than Precious Gems

"If you can find a truly good wife, she is worth more than precious gems! Her husband can trust her, and she will richly satisfy his needs. She will not hinder him but help him all her life." (Prov. 31:10–12, TLB)

A Virtuous Woman

"Charm can be deceptive and beauty doesn't last, but a woman who fears and reverences God shall be greatly praised. Praise her for the many fine things she does. These good deeds of hers shall bring her honor and recognition from people of importance." (Prov. 31:30–31, TLB)

Introspection

Be careful in judging or criticizing others without first checking yourself. Even the worst person possesses good attributes, and even the best person possesses bad attributes.

One should not boast, and say what they would never do, because under the **right** circumstances, a person would do the identical thing, or worse, than the person they are criticizing.

> "And why quibble about the speck in someone else's eye—his little fault—when a board is in your own? How can you think of saying to him, 'Brother, let me help you get rid of that speck in your eye,' when you can't see past the board in yours? Hypocrite! First get rid of the board, and then perhaps you can see well enough to deal with his speck!" (Luke 6:41–42, TLB)

Fixing me first, is the first step toward fixing you.

*****

> "Jesus answered and said unto them, 'Though I bear record of myself, yet my record is true: for I know whence I came, and whither I go, but ye cannot tell whence I come, and whither I go.'" (John 8:14, KJV)

The thought: Another person's thoughts are your perception until they are revealed to you. "You don't know another person like they know themselves." It will be more advantageous if you spend more time concentrating on your own origin and destination and less time on another.

*****

"And, behold, there arose a great tempest in the sea, in so much that the ship was covered with the waves: but he was asleep. And his disciples came to him, and awoke him, saying, 'Lord, save us: we perish.' And he saith unto them, 'Why are ye so fearful, O ye of little faith?' Then he arose, and rebuked the wind and the sea and there was a great calm." (Matt. 8:24–26, KJV)

The thought: Making too much ado about nothing. Things are not always the way they appear to the naked eye. Be aware, and be careful. Every eye closed is not asleep!

*****

"And above all things have fervent charity among yourselves: For charity [love] shall cover the multitude of sins." (1 Pet. 4:8, KJV)

The thought: Love has unlimited power.

*****

"Redeeming the time, because the days are evil." (Eph. 5:16, KJV)

The thought: Time waits for no one. It keeps moving on somehow, so if you are ever going to do a good deed or say kind words, do it right now! It just may be, and one day it will be your very last time.

What Time Is It?

"To every thing there is a season, and a time to every purpose under the heaven:

- A time to be born, and a time to die; a time to plant, and a time to pluck up that which is planted;
- A time to kill, and a time to heal; a time to break down, and a time to build up;
- A time to weep, and a time to laugh; a time to mourn, and a time to dance;
- A time to cast away stones, and a time to gather stones together; a time to embrace, and a time to refrain from embracing;
- A time to get, and a time to lose; a time to keep, and a time to cast away;
- A time to rend, and a time to sew; a time to keep silence, and a time to speak;
- A time to love, and a time to hate; a time of war, and a time of peace." (Eccles. 3:1–8, KJV)

The thought: Timing is everything. Make a careful choice, and choose the right time to do it. It's very seldom there can be a wrong way to do the right thing, and rarely, there can be a right way to do the wrong thing. However, there will always be a right time, and a right way to do the right thing.

Did You Know?

_____

That many things you're doing and saying, you are merely repeating what was previously said or done by someone many, many, many years ago?

That "there is nothing new under the sun? Is there anything of which one can say, "Look! This is something new?" It was here already, long ago; it was here before our time." (Eccles. 1:10, NIV)

*****

That a person's life span is set for **seventy** years of age, but a numerous of variables can alter it?

"Our days may come to seventy years, or eighty, if our strength endures; yet the best of them are but trouble and sorrow, for they quickly pass, and we fly away." (Ps. 90:10, NIV)

*****

That the jail cell was the first automatic door to open, and Peter was the first man to walk through it.

"Peter therefore kept in prison: but prayer was made without ceasing of the church unto God for him... And, behold, the angel of the Lord came upon him, and a light shined in the prison: and he smote Peter on the side, and raised him up, saying, 'Arise up quickly.' And his chains fell off from his hands… When they were past the first and second ward, they came into the iron gate that leadeth into the city; which opened to them of his own accord: and they went out, and passed on through one street; and forthwith the angel departed from him." (Acts 12:5, 7, 10, KJV)

*****

That with the right person, under the right command and for the right reason, will an axe head swim? How do you differentiate between a loan and a gift? If it's a gift, receive it with joy, but if it's a loan, by all mean, you must pay it back, no matter the circumstances.

"But as one of them was chopping, his axhead fell into the river. 'Oh, sir,' he cried, "it was borrowed!" 'Where did it fall?' the prophet asked. The youth showed him the place, and Elisha cut a stick and threw it into the water; and the axhead rose to the surface and floated! 'Grab it,' Elisha said to him; and he did." (2 King 6:5-7, TLB)

*****

That a fish was the first to issue an automatic cash withdrawal? It was called the "Capernaum First Fish National Automated Teller Mouth." (ATM)

"Notwithstanding, lest we should offend them [tax collectors—*IRS*], go thou to the sea, and cast an hook, and take up the **fish** that **first** cometh up; and when thou hast opened his mouth [or account], thou shalt find a piece of money: that take [or withdraw], and give unto them [*tax collectors*] for me and thee." (Matt. 17:27, KJV)

*****

That Adam was the first patient to receive an operation?

"And the Lord God caused a deep sleep to fall upon Adam, and he slept: and he took one of his ribs, and **closed up** (sewed) the flesh instead thereof." (Gen. 2:21, KJV)

*****

That God performed the first wedding?

"And the rib, which the Lord God had taken from man, made he a woman and brought her to Adam." God walked his daughter, Eve, the bride down the aisle and gave her away to Adam, the groom. (Gen. 2:22, KJV)

*****

That God performed the first heart transplant and no one had to die for the recipient to receive it?

"A **new heart** also will I give you, and a new spirit will I put within you: and I will take away the stony heart out of your flesh, and I will give you an heart of flesh. And I will put my spirit within you, and cause you to walk in my statutes, and ye shall keep my judgment, and do them." (Ezek. 36:26–27, KJV)

Our Golden Year

May 10, 1969-2019

PAST

My wife and I have creatively celebrated our Wedding Anniversaries in numerous ways. Some of our favorites have been resort getaways along the beautiful coastal waterways of Washington State and relaxing in picturesque hotels that dot the Oregon Coast bordered by the Pacific Ocean to the west and the Oregon Coast Range to the east. We've spent pleasurable moments in Vancouver and Victoria, British Columbia (Canada), and for our Twentieth Wedding Anniversary, in 1989, I surprised Mary Alice with a trip to Honolulu, Hawaii.

When we celebrated our forty-eighth Wedding Anniversary in May of 2017, I suggested to Mary Alice that we celebrate our Fiftieth Anniversary by going back to West Monroe, Louisiana, where we met and fell in love. Call me a hopeless romantic, but I wanted to share with my bride and celebrate with our family, former classmates from Richardson High School, and the neighborhood friends of West Monroe, the enduring love Mary Alice and I have enjoyed for five decades.

My love said she would think about it and let me know. A few weeks went by, and we decided to wait to make a decision when we were closer to our Golden Anniversary. I wasn't disappointed at the delay, I knew however we decided to celebrate, it would be wonderful!

PRESENT

Coby—Grandpa   Cedric—Daughter, Imani

Carisa—"Never Forgotten"

In November of 2017, Joyce Ann Hanspard-Hewitt, Mary Alice's former Richardson High School classmate and friend came for a visit from Glenn Heights, Texas for Thanksgiving. During a casual conversation, Mary Alice mentioned the subject to Joyce about my suggestion of celebrating our Fiftieth Wedding Anniversary in West Monroe on May 10, 2019. Joyce thought it was a unique and beautiful suggestion, and would be delighted to help in any way she could.

The Green Light

Joyce's enthusiasm motivated Mary Alice to accept my suggestion, so we proceeded to make plans to celebrate our anniversary in West Monroe. The planning was just as memorable as the event. We discussed in detail how we wanted to commemorate our fifty years of commitment through the valleys and rivers of life. Our vow to love each other for better, for worse, for richer, for poorer, in sickness and health, until death do us part had been lived out between us through the good and the bad. Also, this celebration would represent our praise to God for blessing and helping us every step of the way.

Mary Alice and I decided on a weekend event that would begin on the day of our anniversary, Friday, May 10, 2019. Surrounded by family and friends, we would renew our vows at the West Monroe Convention Center. Saturday would be a special day for ourselves, and on Sunday, May 12th we would host an Appreciation Picnic to express our gratitude to the guests who traveled from near and far to help us celebrate our Golden Wedding Anniversary.

In May of 2018, we compiled a guest list of attendees. The list included family, former classmates who attended Richardson High School, and friends from the old neighborhoods. After networking to retrieve addresses, the next step was to mail out the *Save The Date Notices* informing the invitees of our desire for them to join us in celebrating our *Fiftieth Wedding Anniversary.* The save the date notices were mailed out in June.

Mary Alice and I agreed that at least seventy-five people needed to confirm attending to proceed with the event. Shortly after mailing the Save The Date Notices we received phone calls and many responses via mail from invitees all over the country. They expressed how privileged and elated they felt to be invited and would be in attendance.

In January of 2019, we mailed the invitations to the guests. I must admit I was anxious as I waited for the anticipated RSVPs from the majority of the guests confirming they would attend.

By the end of April, we received approximately one hundred and fifty RSVPs! Mary Alice and I were overwhelmed at the thought that we were loved by so many people who wanted to be a part of our celebration. Excitement doesn't begin to describe how we felt as we counted off the days. May 10th could not come soon enough! We were thrilled to have the chance to see family, friends, and classmates we had not seen in over fifty years.

The Departure

On Monday, May 6th Mary Alice and I along with my brothers, Larry and Lee Sampson, Mary Alice's nephew, Kevin Calcote, and his wife Allison flew to West Monroe to finalize preparations for the celebration. Departing a few days later was my son, Cedric, grandson, Jacoby, granddaughter, Imani, and Mary Alice's nephew, Derrick Manning, along with a host of other family members, including Delores Grace, a friend of the family for about forty-five years. There was a total of twenty-eight people who traveled from the State of Washington to attend our joyous event.

Mary Alice and I felt blessed, honored and humble after learning of the vast number of people traveling from all parts of the United States, who was ecstatic to share this milestone with us. The celebration convened on *Friday, May 10th* at West Monroe Convention Center as planned, with the Renewal of Vows Ceremony, followed by dinner and a program. It concluded on *Sunday, May 12th*, with the Appreciation Picnic for our guests at Kiroli Park in West Monroe.

The Ceremony

Just before the start of the ceremony, I took a moment to gaze across the beautifully decorated room. The simple elegance of the setting was beyond my expectation. The décor colors were classic gold, ivory, and shades of blue. Mary Alice chose blue because it is my favorite color. The chairs were covered in ivory with gold bow tie sashes. Flower arrangements echoed the color theme and were artfully arranged in gold trumpet vases and on gold pedestal stands. The tables were covered with ivory dinner-length table cloths. They were accented with twenty-inch gold crystal chandelier centerpieces, and eighteen-inch gold crystal tulip candle holders which sat on gold ruffled cloth and plastic chargers.

The Renewal Wedding Party consisted of the following:

Matron of Honor	Moira Chung (our goddaughter, Carisa' god sister)
Bridesmaids	Paula Jefferson (Family Friend)
	Imani E. Sampson (Granddaughter)
Flower Girl	Nyla Brown (Great Niece)
Best Man	Cedric A. Sampson (Son)
Groomsmen	Jacoby N. A. Sampson (Grandson)
	Naim Brown (Great Nephew)
Ring Bearer	Nissir Brown (Great Nephew)
Candle-lighters	Anetria Sampson-Green (Niece)
	Kevin Calcote (Nephew)

Note: Our Granddaughter, Janahya N. Sampson, and Great Granddaughter, Harmoney Basa were not able to attend the events.

Special thanks to Pastor William Cann, Joyce Hanspard-Hewitt, my brothers, Lee and Larry, my sister, Mary C. Sampson, Mary Alice's brother and sister, Willie E. Manning, Vassie L. Manning-Watson, her nephew, Derrick Manning, cousin, Willie L. "Josh" Manning, and niece, Allison Calcote. Also, we would like to give special thanks to my cousins, Hardy Gunn, Elaine Hicks-Ross and Diane Coleman-Jacobs. Shout-outs to: Sue Britton, Dorothy McNeal, Bobbie Johnson-Clay, and to Nick Roberson for filling in at the last minute, without giving it a second thought. You all were so kind and willingly agreed to participate on the program.

The Renewal of Vows Ceremony was amazingly beautiful and emotional. I think I may have cried through the entire renewal of the vows. It was as if I was marrying Mary Alice for the first time. I don't know why, but during our first marriage ceremony, I was not as emotional as I was this time. *However, it was all good.*

The ceremony began with the candle lighters performing their duty and then the clergy and gentlemen entered the room. I was excited but not nearly as nervous as I thought I would be. There were two reasons for my excitement: One, I was only a few minutes away from renewing my vows with the woman I have loved and been married to for *fifty years!* Secondly, the mystery of not knowing who was in attendance. Although we had numerous RSVPs, I still didn't know if everyone had been able to make it to the event.

I followed approximately six feet behind the minister as he made his way to the platform where the ceremony was to take place. Right behind me were Cedric, Jacoby, Naim, and Nissir in that order. As I entered the room, I glanced to my left at the crowded room of approximately one hundred and twenty-five people. I was thrilled to see a couple of former classmates from Richardson High School. I continued to follow the minister, looking straight ahead as I suddenly became self-conscious of the many eyes that were watching me. I stayed focused and refrained from scanning the room.

Once the Renewal Wedding Party was in place, all eyes turned to Mary Alice as she entered the room, stepping to the beat of the song, *"Tonight I Celebrate My Love,"* by Roberta Flack and Peabo Bryson. A song she selected because she said, *"All of the words express how I feel about you."* Mary Alice smiled beautifully as she graciously took each step in her floor-length ivory-sequenced gown, ivory tiara and rose wedding veil hat. Unashamed tears flowed as I watched my bride walk down the aisle. She was more than beautiful; she was breathtaking!

The entire ceremony was a roller coaster ride of emotions for me. I remember reaching for Mary Alice's hands just before we said our vows. I watched as she slowly placed her hands into mine, and then we gazed into each other's eyes as we begin our vows and listened to the song she dedicated to me, *"You Make Me Feel Brand New"* by the Stylistics and the songs I dedicated to her, *"Endless Love"* by Diana Ross and Lionel Richie and *"Thank You For Your Love"* by the Dramatics.

Mary Alice and I were going back and forth in trying to select the perfect song for our special dance. The ideal song would capture our fifty-plus years of love, in a nutshell. One day Cedric, our son, came to visit. Entering the house in a euphoria mood, as if he could not hold it any longer, Cedric said, "Mom, Dad I found the perfect song for your special dance during the Wedding Vows Renewal Ceremony!"

Cedric continued and said the name of the song is You and I, by Stevie Wonder. The three of us immediately rushed to the commuter and Googled the song. Mary Alice and I were sold after listening to the first couple of stanzas. This came as no surprise to Cedric for he knew the words spoke volume to the love we share. The song captured the essence of our knitted souls. The fact that our son selected this song for us made it even more heartwarming.

At the appropriate time, we slowly made our way to the dance floor at the sweet sound of the music, You and I.

I embraced Mary Alice and she embraced me in return. It was very emotional and difficult to hold back the tears as the words from the song found their way to our ears and pierced our hearts.

"You and I (We Can Conquer the World)"

Here we are on earth together, It's you and I.

God has made us fall in love it's true, I really found someone like you.

Will it stay the love you feel for me, will it say, that you will be by my side to see me through, until my life is through.

Well in my mind we can conquer the world. In love you and I, you and I, you and I.

I am glad at least in my life I found someone, That may not be here forever to see me through, But I found strength in you.

I only pray that I have shown you a brighter day, Because that's all that I am living for you see.

Don't worry what happens to me, Cause in my mind you will stay here always. In love you and I, you and I, you and I.

You and, ohhhhh, in my mind we can conquer the world. In love you and I, you and I, you and I.!!!

At the halfway point of the song, we asked our guests to join us as we celebrate our special, momentous moment.

It thrilled our hearts as we glanced around the room and observed family, friends and former classmates partaking in our joy while giving the appearance of savoring the *never again opportunity*. **UNFORGETTABLE!**

Overwhelming love filled the room during and after the ceremony as family members, friends, and former classmates embraced each other with tightly squeezed hugs and firm handshakes. Of course, reminiscing about the good old days was one of the main topics. There were so many people from the old neighborhoods and high school classmates that it felt like a mini family/school reunion!

Doug Seegers, the Director of Parks & Recreation for the City of West Monroe put *the icing on the cake* when he stepped to the podium and presented us with a Proclamation on behalf of the Mayor of the City, Staci Mitchell. Also, from the Mayor's Office, Doug presented me with a Certificate of Appreciation for my dedication and many years of service as the Founder and President of the Haynes Lane Bonded By Love Community Reunion.

The Haynes Lane Bonded
By Love Community

The Haynes Lane Community was a very close-knit community. We hung out, laughed, cried together, played on the neighborhood softball and baseball teams from the time we were about twelve years old until age nineteen. Artis Wilson organized our first softball team in 1961.

My dad, the late Eddie J. Sampson took over as softball coach in 1962 after Artis enlisted in the Air Force. He later taught us how to play baseball, as well. He changed the name of the team from *the Lane Softball Team* to the *West Monroe Jets,* AKA, *the Jets.* My brothers Lee and Eddie Dean, AKA, Dean were members of the team. We played both, softball and baseball games against teams in other communities. During my dad's coaching tenure, we were crowned the East Monroe (often referred to as Monroe) Baseball League Champions in 1962.

The Ouachita River separates Monroe from West Monroe. Two bridges join the two cities. The name of one is the Louisville Avenue Bridge, which was also called the *New Bridge*. It is currently called the Lea Joyner Bridge, renamed in her honor due to her years of ministry on the bank of the river. Lea Joyner was an ordained woman Methodist Pastor. In 1952 she established a mission between the Levee and the Ouachita River that served the very poor residents. On March 12, 1985, an emotionally disturbed young man who she attempted to help murdered her.

Just south of the Louisville Avenue Bridge is the Endom Bridge, namely, the DeSiard Street Bridge or the Old Bridge. It was dedicated in 1899 and named after Judge Robert and Mayor Fred Endom. During that time, to gain access to the two cities was via one of the two bridges.

Besides Monroe Baseball Summer League, we also competed in West Monroe baseball summer league and was crowned Champions. On the days we had games, the girls, most of whom were our girlfriends, cheered us on. When the girls had games, we would support them. During the home games, the "home field advantage" was in full effect as the adults lined up on the sides of the softball field and cheered wildly for us; win or lose. My dad also coached the girls' softball team.

My girlfriend, Mary Alice along with her sisters, Alice, AKA, Alice Mae and the late Dorothy Ann, AKA, Dot, were members of the team. Their brother, Isaac James Manning, AKA, Brother or Bro, was a player on the Jets' Team. Also, my sisters, Peggy and Corinthia, AKA, Faye were fellow teammates on the girls' team. Having been born in a very athletic family, evidently the talent was in the DNA, inherited from our father and uncles.

The girls' team was awesome, endowed with skillful players in every position. Their toughest competitors were the teams from the Quarters and Trenton Community. Both teams had exceptional players as well. Still, after many years removed from the ball diamond, all three teams lay claim to being the best team. But of course, perhaps with just a tad bias, my wife and I yet cling to the truth that the Lane Girls' Softball Team was the best team in West Monroe.

If the adults observed misbehavior, we got chastised. It didn't matter if they were a relative or not. Parenting, in those days, extended beyond your children and embraced every kid in the neighborhood; always in love and genuine concern. Afterward, our parents were made aware of the situation. Disciplinary actions were taken at that time by our parents. The disciplinary action was distributed based on the severity of the misconduct. My dad coached until he became terminal ill, subsequently passing on Thursday, March 12, 1964.

The Birth of the Haynes Lane Bonded by Love Community Reunion

_____

Although I'd been away from my community for many years, the love we had for each other never died. I decided to contact the former Lane residents to inquire if they would be interested in reuniting in a Haynes Lane Community Reunion. I received overwhelmingly positive responses in favor of the reunion. In July of 1996, the Haynes Lane Bonded By Love Community Reunion Organization was formed. Past residents traveled from near and far to attend. It was a beautiful sight to behold. Reuniting with former residents, friends and teammates were breathtaking, to say the least.

The Reunion was so amazing it was held for three consecutive years, 1996, 1997, and 1998. After that, it was held every two years and drew a crowd of approximately *300 to 500* people during the three-day festivities. It was such a success that Mayor Dave Norris Sr., Mayor of the City of West Monroe presented us with a Permanent Proclamation, proclaiming *July 2nd* to *July 7th* as the Haynes Lane Bonded By Love Community Reunion Week. Dave Norris Sr. held his position of Mayor for the City of West Monroe for forty years, from 1978 until 2018 at which time his successor, Staci Mitchell took office on July 1, 2018.

The Forbidden Territory

Now let me get back to the Golden Wedding Anniversary. Reuniting with family, friends, and classmates was a wonderful feeling. There were former classmates in attendance who Mary Alice and I had not seen since we graduated over fifty years ago. Included were former football and baseball teammates who played with me during the various seasons and contributed to the Richardson High school Bears advancing to the State final three consecutive years. We were the AA State Runner-up in the *1965-1966 season*, and State Champions two consecutive years, during the *1966-1967 season* and the *1967-1968 season*. Also, there were former basketball teammates present, and friends who had performed as cheerleaders with Mary Alice.

On a side note: Richardson High School '67-'68 football team set a school record for being the first Black school to participate in any activity at a predominant Southern White School. Our team was set to play the Northwestern Braves of Zachary, Louisiana in the State Championship game. The game was scheduled to be played at Richardson High School Stadium, (our home field) but the School's Principal, the late James L. Thomas (A.K.A., Coach Thomas), Head Coach, the late Elvin Spears, and Assistant Coach, the late Sam Burns were concerned that the stadium could not accommodate the expected sellout crowd. Therefore arrangements were made for the game to be played at West Monroe High School Rebels' Stadium.

As I aforementioned, West Monroe High School was predominantly a white school, consisting of all white students and faculty. This was during the time of segregation in which the *Negroes* were expected, sternly warned and forced to, *"Stay in your place."* The Negroes' (AKA, *"Colored People"*) place was limited to drinking from the **Colored Only** water fountain, utilizing the **Colored Only** restrooms, and *grubbing out* (dining) in the **Colored Only** café or diner, as if our skin color was contagious. I could go on and on with this subject, but I will simplify it by saying the Colored People's place was the direct opposite of the White People's Domain. The White People's Domain consisted of *predominately* White People and loaded with the best of everything. I did not lose any sleep wondering how "Coach" Thomas pulled off *the barely short of a miracle feat*, I was just thrilled to get an opportunity to play on a football field that was a predominantly White School's Stadium. I just knew their stadium was a lot more intriguing than ours. So be it, if the School's Mascot was/is, Rebels. I had no qualms about playing on the Rebel's Field, even though it was deemed taboo, or forbidden to do so, during the time. It was for that reason alone, I found extra motivation to play the game on their field, despite the extreme prejudice and racism demonstrated.

The game was played on Friday, December 8, 1967, there were approximately two thousand (2,000) people in attendance. To my surprise, I looked into the crowd and spotted a few white students and adults as well, among the mostly black supporters. The nervousness I felt about the "big game" and possibly the final game of my career (I was a senior) became secondary because up to that point I had never played in front of a crowd as large as this. During the pre-game warm-up, I was yet in awe at the thought of playing the game at West Monroe High School Stadium. But just before Kickoff my focus shifted to the **big game**. At that time my major adversary (at least for approximately the next two hours) was the opposing team, the Northwestern Braves, and not the other race. I say this because Northwestern was a very good football team. We anticipated a valiant effort from them, in their quest to dethrone the Bears. They ended their regular season with a 10-0 record and were the South Division Champions. Richardson's regular-season record was 8-1 and the North Division Champions. Our only blemish was to a Powerhouse AAA team, the Richwood High School Rams, located in Monroe. We finished the season with a combined 12-1 record.

As far as the game, we came out victorious, defeating Northwestern by a score of 19-18, crowning the Richardson High School Bears State Champions. The record-setter came, and I stand to be corrected, but it is my belief that Richardson High School

Bears 1967-1968 football team was the first to set foot on the Rebels' soil, or compete on any Southern White School's soil during the era of segregation.

Also, I believe that other than the 1967-1968 *"Bears"* Football Team there are no other teams, black or white who has won a Championship Game on the Rebels' field in any era. The *"Bears" yet hold those records,* to boot. The 1967–1968 "Bears" was the last team to win a State Championship at Richardson High School. In 1970 students were bused to West Monroe High School as part of the desegregation process for that area. Richardson High School was transitioned to a Junior High School. A few years later the junior high school was closed. The school is presently converted to an alternative school. Additionally, the Ouachita Parish School Board Office is housed at the school. *"Food For Thought Only."*

With the deepest passion, I must mention that my favorite coach was the late Donell Cowan, who held the position of Assistant Coach. Also, other teammates claimed Coach Cowan as their favorite coach. Coach Cowan resigned from his coaching position at Richardson High School before the '67-'68 football season to become Head Coach for the Grambling High School Kittens.

Now back to the celebration. There were many places, Mary Alice, and I could have chosen to celebrate our Golden Wedding Anniversary: Such as a romantic getaway to Paris, France or a cruise to St. Croix which would have been a great choice, but instead decided to return to West Monroe, our humble beginning where it all started. By doing so, we were able to share this milestone with family, friends, and former classmates from Richardson High School. Even though we live thousands of miles away, we yet love our city and the community that took part in raising us.

We've Only Just Begun

Our motto was, "*Going Back In Time To Recapture The Moment,*" and inviting family and friends who were a part of "that moment" (our courtship days). We chose the slogan, "*Fifty Years Done, And We've Only Just Begun.*" Celebrating our Golden Wedding Anniversary in this manner was very important because we never forgot our roots, and could not think of a better place, or better people to help celebrate this special occasion other than our family, former classmates of Richardson High School, and friends from the neighborhoods of West Monroe.

The weekend event was SIMPLY AMAZING! If it was possible we would have frozen the moment for weeks. We really hated to see it all come to an end. *It was a blast, a pleasant weekend to remember for a lifetime.*

Epilogue

Thoughts is a book that is filled with many positive statements and provides solutions to diverse problems. If applied correctly, the thoughts and proverbs in this book will ensure a positive impact on one's life. Affecting lives is Charles and Mary Alice's passion, goal, and vision. I have no doubt God has equipped and called them for that sole purpose. Charles is committed to the point that he purchased two T-shirts that have the words, *"Born to Make a Difference"* personalized on the front. Also, personalized on the front of another shirt are the words, *"Born to Shine Since '49"* (1949 is Charles's birth year).

Charles and his daughter, the late Carisa, are the founders of Jacob's Ladder Community Resource Center (JLCRC). JLCRC is a 501(c)(3) nonprofit business that provides a variety of services to assist those who are in need. Mary Alice has a vital role of coordinating the services provided.

Charles has received numerous awards for providing outstanding service to the communities. The tremendous impact he had on many people's lives made a vast difference in who they are today. To name a few of the awards he received: Recipient for Outstanding Public Service, and the Most Inspirational from the Seattle Police Department; The Law Enforcement Achievement Recognition Award from the National Center for Mission and Exploited Children; Outstanding Volunteer Award from KUBE (FM) Radio Station; Father of the Year Recipient; and many more for affecting people's lives in a positive manner.

Charles and Mary Alice are a good team. Charles is the strength to Mary Alice's weakness, and she is the strength to his weakness. Carisa would often say to them, "Mom, Dad, it takes two of you to make one." Carisa is absolutely correct. Separately they are vulnerable, but together, they are a force to be reckoned with.

This book speaks volumes of the positive impact that Charles and Mary Alice impart into people's lives on a constant basis.

L to R: Cedric, Imani, Mary Alice, Charles,
Jacoby, Derrick D. Manning (Nephew)

Mary Alice & Charles

Hangin Out With Grandma in Louisiana

PECANLAND MALL
MONROE, LOUISIANA

Enjoying An Outing With My Dad

CEDRIC AND FAMILY

Harmoney, (Granddaughter) Imani, Janahya, Cedric

Coby Receiving Love From Mom (Carisa)

Janahya—Dad

Harmoney (age 5)
(Janahya's Daughter)

Imani (age 11)

Imani age 16 (Present)

Imani age (Present)

Coby—Mom

"INSEPARABLE"
Carisa, the Heart—Jacoby, the Heartbeat

Coby—Imani

Coby—Janahya

Cedric—Carisa

Siblings Love On Easter Sunday, April 20, 2014

"MY HERO"

WALT DISNEY WORLD
ORLANDO, FLORIDA

Carisa Hangin With 'Lil Coby

Feelin Secure With Mommy

Cousins Bond

Grandpa's Hands

Sisters

Sandwiched Between Love

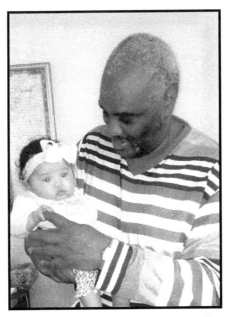

Baby Harmoney Meets Great Grandpa

"ALL MY CHILDREN"

Great-Niece, Baby Harmoney, Janahya, Imani, Carisa

About the Authors

Charles was born in Monroe, Louisiana, and raised in West Monroe, Louisiana. Mary Alice was born in Ruston, Louisiana, and also raised in West Monroe. Charles is the third of eleven children born to the late Eddie and Essie Mae Sampson. He has a niece who is like a sister to him and his siblings. She was raised in their household from birth. Mary Alice is the fourth of ten children born to the late John and Charity Manning.

Charles and Mary Alice were elementary school sweethearts. The courtship began when they were fifteen. The courtship ended on May 10, 1969, when they were united in matrimony.

They migrated to Seattle, Washington, in November 1969, along with their six-month-old son, Cedric Antoine Sampson. On December 1, 1970, they were blessed with a daughter, the late Carisa Nicole Jacquette Sampson.

Charles was employed by the Seattle Police Department as a Community Service Officer. He retired on January 1, 2009, after thirty-seven years of service. Mary Alice was employed by the City of Seattle as an Administrative Staff Analyst. She retired in May 2008.

They are blessed with a grandson, Jacoby Nicholas Antoine Sampson, two granddaughters, Janahya Naquise Sampson and Imani Elizabeth Sampson, one great-granddaughter, Harmoney Basa. The couple are the ideal role model to their family and others who cross their path.

Love, compassion, patience, and faith in God are just a small part of their virtues. As born again believers, and filled with the Holy Ghost, their priorities are to walk in the Spirit immensely, to ensure that their lives are a reflection of the Godhead that resides within. They find fulfillment and joy in making a difference in people's lives in a positive manner. Charles and Mary Alice have dedicated their lives to serving others, with little thought for their well-being.

NOTES

NOTES

NOTES

CPSIA information can be obtained
at www.ICGtesting.com
Printed in the USA
BVHW020941250821
615155BV00002B/1/J